PURITAN PREACHING IN ENGLAND

A STUDY OF PAST AND PRESENT

THE LYMAN BEECHER LECTURES ON PREACHING AT YALE UNIVERSITY, OCTOBER, 1899

PURITAN PREACHING IN ENGLAND

A Study of Past and Present

BY

JOHN BROWN, B.A., D.D.

AUTHOR OF "JOHN BUNYAN, HIS LIFE, TIMES, AND WORK," "THE PILGRIM FATHERS AND THEIR PURITAN SUCCESSORS," ETC.

Wipf and Stock Publishers

150 West Broadway • Eugene OR 97401

2001

Puritan Preaching in England
A Study of Past and Present

By Brown, John

ISBN: 1-57910-752-4

Reprinted by *Wipf and Stock Publishers*
150 West Broadway • Eugene OR 97401

Previously published by Charles Scribner's Sons, 1900.

TO THE

REV. GEORGE P. FISHER, D.D., LL.D.

Professor of Ecclesiastical History and Dean
of the Faculty of Theology in
Yale University,

IN GRATEFUL REMEMBRANCE OF A PLEASANT
AND GREATLY VALUED FRIENDSHIP.

CONTENTS.

I

INTRODUCTORY — THE PREACHING OF THE FRIARS

LECTURE I

INTRODUCTORY—THE PREACHING OF THE FRIARS

GENTLEMEN OF THE DIVINITY SCHOOL:

IN entering upon the series of Lectures I begin to-day let me do so with a preliminary word of personal sort. When a preacher consents to lecture on Preaching he is very apt to be haunted by a fear lest that consent should be interpreted to mean that he presents himself as an example of the ideal he is about to hold up to others. Lest my consent to speak to you should be so construed let me hasten at once to shelter myself behind the modest words with which even so great a Church Father as Augustine felt it needful to conclude the fourth book of his treatise on Christian Doctrine. This work, intended as a manual for preachers, thus concludes: "I give thanks to God that with what little ability I possess I have in these four books striven to depict not the sort of man I am myself (for my defects are very many), but the sort of man he ought to be who desires to labor in sound, that is, in Christian doctrine, not for his own instruction only, but for that of others also."

The men who have been longest engaged in the work of preaching will be those most ready to understand the feeling expressed in these words. They are painfully conscious how imperfectly they have been able to realize their own ideal. For the work of the Christian ministry grows greater to our thought the longer we are in it, and with this growing sense of the greatness of the work there comes a deepening consciousness of our own insufficiency for it. One of the greatest — perhaps the greatest — personality in the pulpit of English Congregationalism during the forty years between 1829 and 1869 was Thomas Binney, the well-known pastor of the Weigh House Church in London. During the years I have mentioned he not only largely shaped the character of some of our foremost laymen, but also inaugurated a new era of preaching for the younger generation of preachers. Year after year students for the Christian Ministry gathered round that far-famed pulpit to catch the living inspiration he gave them for their own life-work. Among those often found there in that earlier time was one now known on both sides the Atlantic as the great Manchester preacher — Alexander Maclaren. Indulging in some early reminiscences on the occasion of his Jubilee as a minister, he spoke of Thomas Binney as "the man that taught me to preach." He went on to say: "I remember when once, with the enthusiasm of the student, I went to him to thank him for all that I had learned from him, he said to me with tears in his eyes — 'Don't speak about it! It's all such a poor thing — it's all such a poor thing.'" After being for fifty years a preacher himself, Dr. Maclaren said, "I understand his point of view now as I did not then." In like manner the late Dr. Dale after preaching Christ's Gospel to his people for forty years, wrote to them at the end of that time, saying: "It seems to me sometimes that I am only just beginning to catch a faint glimpse of the glory and power of the redemption which God has wrought for us through the Incarnation, Death, Resurrection, and Ascension of our Lord Jesus Christ."

When the invitation came to me to deliver the present series of the Lyman Beecher Lecture, there came with it the suggestion that some historical theme such as Puritan Preaching (or Preachers) would be well within the scope of the Founder's purpose. To speak quite frankly, this suggestion really decided me to consent to come to you. For I could not but remember how many and comprehensive have been the counsels of those who have preceded me in this Lectureship; with what practical wisdom they have treated such subjects as the training and equipment of the preacher, the preparation and delivery of the sermon; and the best methods of conducting church worship and church affairs. I remembered, too, what earnest words have again and again been spoken on such still closer matters as that of the divine call in the preacher's own soul, and the watchful heed he must needs keep over his own spiritual life. I felt that I could not hope to add anything of value to what had been already so powerfully said by so many distinguished men both from your side of the Atlantic and ours. But when the subject of Puritan Preachers and Preaching was suggested to me, it seemed, first of all, to fall in with a line of study which has always been pleasant to me; next that it would be somewhat of a variation from lines previously travelled; and finally that something might be gained to the present by a brief historical review of the preaching of the past, and of the forces which made it what it was.

Such review will, I venture to think, tend to deepen your own sense of the importance of the work in which your own life is to be spent. In any department of service it is good for the worker himself to feel that the work to be done has always been felt to be well worth the doing. And he who realizes the living place which preaching, in its most vital forms, has ever taken in the spiritual life of the Church will need no further assurance of its great importance. He will not fail to note that the preacher's message and the Church's spiritual condition have risen or fallen together. When life has gone out of the preacher it is not long before it has gone out of the Church also. On the other hand, when there has been a revived message of life on the preacher's lips there comes as a consequence a revived condition in the Church itself. The connection between these two things has been close, uniform, and constant.

Such a look-back as I propose to take may also serve, I think, to quicken a holy ambition. The least and lowliest may be transfigured and heightened by the grandeur of inherited associations; and if it be so, the Christian preacher may well be inspired with a noble enthusiasm. For as he looks back into the past he finds himself standing in the ranks with men of the most varied ability, and with many of the highest genius, who have consecrated their powers to this high and noble service. It has been well said that there is true stimulus to be gained from the greatest masters of speech dealing with the greatest of all themes — God, the soul, eternity, sin, salvation, Christ. And it may well fill the humblest worker in the vineyard with a just and holy ambition to do his best in this high service, by God's help, and to prove himself not unworthy.

Then, too, a brief historical review not merely of Preaching, but of Puritan Preaching in England may have one other advantage in this place. It may serve to strengthen those bonds of brotherhood between America and England which of recent years have been growing so much closer, to the joy of all right-minded and God-fearing men. For it can scarcely fail to remind us of our oneness as a people, not merely in our Anglo-Saxon speech and lineage, but also in the deepest and most sacred things of all. The makers of New England were what they were in holy courage and splendid daring for God and truth, because before they reached the New England shores they had sat side by side in the old parish churches of England, and listened to the same Puritan sermons with the men who remained on the other side the sea. Theologically and spiritually the Pilgrim Fathers and Cromwell's Ironsides had a common ancestry. Some of the best elements in your national life as well as ours may be traced to the men of strong faith and masculine intelligence who occupied the English pulpits at the end of the sixteenth and the beginning of the seventeenth century.

In the hope, therefore, that we may gain something of practical guidance and spiritual stimulus as preachers, I will ask you to go back with me into the past. And while the requirements of time and space will necessitate that we keep to one definite line, that of Puritan Preaching and Preachers, I will take leave to give a somewhat wide latitude to the term "Puritan" as meaning thereby those preachers who have laid more stress upon Scripture than upon ecclesiastical institutions. Such men there were even before the days of that Protestantism out of which Puritanism came. It may be well, therefore, to glance briefly at the Preaching Friars of the Middle Ages, and at such men as John Wickliffe and John Colet, who made Protestantism possible, before we reach Puritanism proper.

In a remarkable essay on "The Tendencies of Religious Thought in England," written now more than thirty years ago, by Mark Pattison, then rector of Lincoln College, Oxford, he maintained that we ought to apply the laws of thought and the succession of opinion to the course of English theology. He contended that there is a law of continuity in these things which, whatever we may wish, is never broken off; that the religious opinions prevailing in any given age largely determine, either directly or by way of reaction, those prevailing in the age that follows; and that if we would hold any clue through the maze of the present we cannot neglect those immediate agencies in its production which had their origin in the century previous. This being so, and all will admit that so it is, we shall not be wandering aimlessly in this historic review of Puritan Preaching, if first, by way of introduction, we step back for a moment or two and trace the influences at work in the pre-Reformation Church which were more or less preparing the way for it. If we do so we shall find, I think, there were three movements of considerable significance all bearing on the revival of the preaching function in the Church — the movement initiated by Charles the Great at the beginning of the ninth century; the rise of the Preaching Friars in the thirteenth; and the propaganda carried on by John Wickliffe and his followers in the fourteenth. Let me briefly advert to each of these.

Perhaps the darkest period in the history of the Church is that from the eighth century to the twelfth, when the living voice of the preacher was but rarely and feebly heard, if heard at all. Wherever missionaries labored they were of necessity compelled to preach to the people, but where Christianity had been established for some time, preaching was almost entirely superseded by ceremonial and ritual service. To meet this evil condition of things the vigorous mind of Charlemagne earnestly engaged itself, and among his other schemes for the improvement of his Empire was one for the revival of preaching as the means of religious elevation. The institutions he set forth on this behalf show the importance he attached to the office of the preacher, and at the same time expose the miserable unfitness of the clergy generally for the work needing to be done. In the records of the various Councils of the time, also, we find repeated enactments issued, commanding bishops and presbyters to preach to the people in their own proper tongue; instructing them also to preach diligently the Catholic faith to all the people, and themselves to understand the Lord's Prayer, and expound it to all, that each may know what to ask of God. To help the weaker sort of preachers the Emperor employed Paul Winfried to make a Collection of Homilies from the writings of the Fathers, "culling some flowers from their most pleasant fields;" and these Homilies, one hundred and seventy-six in number, were for generations the main source of pulpit instruction for all. The clergy, the men most concerned, responded with but little zeal to the earnestness of the Emperor. Some of them idly read the passage from the Fathers in the original without taking the trouble to translate it into the language of the people, as it was intended and ordered they should. With but few exceptions the religious teachers of the time occupied themselves with mere ceremonies and superstitious legends of the idlest sort. Such preaching as there was consisted for the most part of mystical and allegorical interpretations of Scripture. The preacher who could only give two or three meanings to a text was looked upon as rather a weak brother. The clerical homiletical canon prescribed at least seven and if possible eight meanings for every passage. Besides the literal meaning they felt themselves bound to give, in addition: the allegorical or parabolic; the tropological or etymological; the anagogic or analogical; the typical or exemplar; the anaphoric or proportional; and the mystical or apocalyptic. As William Tyndale said of such men in later days, they divided the scripture into so many senses that the literal sense had become nothing at all. "Twenty doctors," said he, "expound one text twenty ways, and with an antetheme of half an inch some of them draw a thread nine days long." It was a curious result of their rigid belief in the verbal inspiration of the sacred text that it led them into a condition of mind in which they practically ignored the Scriptures altogether.

At the beginning of the thirteenth century we come to one of the most interesting periods in the history of Latin Christianity, previous to the Reformation — the time of the rise of the Mendicant Orders of Preaching Friars, Dominican and Franciscan. Among the regular clergy actual preaching had fallen into disuse. In theory it had come to be regarded as the special privilege of the bishops, and there were but few of these who had either the gift, the inclination, or the leisure to preach even in the cathedral cities. In the rest of their dioceses their presence was but occasional; and then only in the shape of a progress or visitation of pomp and form rather than for any purpose of popular instruction. For the people the services of the Church took the form of ceremonial and the only general teaching was the ritual.

The earlier monastic orders, the monks who preceded the friars, withdrew themselves from an evil world into the seclusion of the cloister, leaving that world to go on its way while they devoted all their care to the salvation of their own souls, as the one great end of life. It was their business to be the salt of the earth, but they were more concerned to guard the salt from losing its savor than that the earth should be sweetened by it. Meantime while the sacerdotalists within the Church were sleeping, there were anti-sacerdotalists outside who were preparing to give them trouble and rouse them from their slumbers. Secret forces were at work, and soon a cry of distress arose from the clergy that heretics outside the Church were by their teaching drawing the people away from them. There were those connected with this revolutionary movement who held to the creeds of the Church, while rejecting its ritual, and repudiating the sacerdotal authority of the clergy. Bernard found "the churches of Toulouse without people, the people without priests, the priests without respect." There were many who rejected the whole hierarchical and ritual system as well as the priesthood. The virtuous layman, said they, is a priest, while the sanctity of the priest is not in his priesthood but in his life, and transubstantiation in the Eucharist takes place not in the hands of the priest but in the heart of the believer.

It was at this juncture when torpor had seized upon the Church within and revolt was raised against her without, that simultaneously and without concert, in two different countries the Friars Preachers, Dominican and Franciscan entered upon their self-denying career. While not unconscious under how many restrictions and with how many reservations the description may be allowed to stand I am disposed to describe them as Puritans before Puritan times. Gathered from every country and speaking therefore various languages and dialects, Christendom was soon overspread by a host of zealous, active, devoted men whose great aim was the religious instruction and elevation of the people. While within monastic rules and bound by the common vows of chastity, poverty, and obedience, seclusion in a walled-up monastery was no part of their discipline. They were bent, not on fleeing the world, but on subjugating or winning it. Their work was among their fellow-men in village and hamlet, in town and city, in market and camp. One of their founders, St. Francis of Assisi, has been called the John Wesley of the thirteenth century and he and his followers went forth without purse or scrip, relying entirely on the voluntary principle for maintenance. The apostles of poverty and pity and an all-embracing love, they went forth by two and two to build up the ruined Church of God.

Moving about among the people and asking to be allowed to help them, like their Master they had compassion on the multitude and began to teach them many things. Compassion is the strength of the true teacher, and instruction is a work of true compassion. Above all things, these men aimed at being effective preachers, and in the course of the movement we find Hubert de Romanis, General of the Dominican Order, issuing a work, entitled *De Eruditione Prœdicatorum*, in which he speaks of preaching as above the Mass and all liturgical services. "For," says he, "of the Latin Liturgy the laity understand nothing; but they can understand the sermon; and hence by preaching God is glorified in a clearer and more open manner than by any other act of worship." This work of Hubert's on preaching may be described as epoch-making, appearing as it did after long centuries of comparative silence. It sets forth to the members of the Order the obligation under which they were placed to preach the Gospel; the gravity and dignity of this great work; and the qualifications necessary for its effective discharge. Of all spiritual exercises in which monks employed themselves, preaching was set forth as the highest, and whoever possessed the talent for it, was bound to cultivate it to the utmost. Hubert points out that when once Christ had commenced preaching, He spent His whole life at that employment; and from this he argued what great effects might be produced in their own times; and maintained that the crowds who followed some of those who did preach showed that the people were ready to receive the spoken message of truth.

While thus urging the importance of preaching he also set before the members of the Order the most effective way of doing it, and the best way of making the most of themselves as preachers. "Though," says he, "the talent for preaching is obtained through the special gift of God, yet the wise preacher will do his own part of the work, and diligently study that he may preach correctly." He warns the brethren against making a mere display of their own ingenuity and eloquence, as, for example, deriving the theme of their discourse from a text altogether foreign to the matter in hand. Such devices, he thinks, are more likely to excite derision than promote edification. As for those who looked more to fine words than true and noble thoughts, they seemed to him to be like people who were more concerned to display their beautiful dishes than to provide food for their guests. Looking through this book of his, we find, as we might expect, that human nature was very much the same then as now. Then as now there were impressible and shallow hearers who had no root in themselves. Many heard the word of God with great delight, but it was only as if they were listening to a beautiful song. Others were kindled to momentary glow to little purpose, for after the sermon they became immediately cold again. We find too from Hubert's book that the ancestors of some of our present-day critics were already to the fore. Others, said he, are, or think they are, good judges of preaching. He has spoken well or ill, say they. Shaking their wise heads over the sermon, they pronounced it too long or too short, too abstruse or too trivial. But though these illuminati of the thirteenth century never failed to criticise the sermon, there was one thing he said they never did — they never applied what was said to their own lives.

It serves further to illustrate the awakened interest in oral and vernacular teaching in those times when we find the abbot of a monastery, Guibert of Novigentum, also writing a book on the best method of preaching, and declaring it to be the general duty of all Christians, and not of bishops only, to labor for the advancement of the Christian life in others, according to the proportion of each man's knowledge and gifts. In this work he urges the preacher to have respect to the wants of the simple and uneducated, as well as the better educated, and to strive in his preaching to unite depth with lucidity and plainness of meaning. Both intellect and heart should be united in this great work. Also says he: "Let the sermon be preceded by prayer; so that the soul, fired with divine love, may utter forth what it feels of God with glowing words; so that the preacher, as he burns in his own heart, may enkindle a flame also in the hearts of his hearers." He would have the preacher enter into the very souls of men, track sin through all its meshes of deceitfulness and show them to themselves. "The preacher," he says, "should treat concerning the motions of the inner man. This was a thing so common to the experience of all men that such a sermon should be obscure to none." Every man could read in his heart, written as it were in a book, what the preacher told him of the various kinds of temptation. No sermon he held to be more useful than that which showed men to themselves, and led back to the secret recesses of their own hearts those who, by the distraction of outward things had become strangers to themselves, presenting their own selves as in a mirror before their own eyes. Heart-experience on the part of the preacher is, he says, his best equipment for speaking to the hearts of others. As he who has been in the heat and fierceness of the battle knows more about it than he who has only heard about it from others, so is it in spiritual warfare. He whose own deepest inward consciousness bears witness to the words he speaks will be able to deal with spiritual conflicts with an altogether different sort of authority from the man who only repeats what he has heard, and he can lay his finger on the precise inward details of the soul.

It is clear from the facts which have come down to us that great moral and spiritual effects resulted from the preaching of the Friars in the earlier, that is, the better days of the movement. We read, for example, of the Franciscan Berthold, a sort of John the Baptist preacher of repentance in the cities of Augsburg and Regensburg. From Thuringia to Bavaria and far into Switzerland he travelled as a herald of the truth. First in one city and then in another he was invited to preach till at length no church was large enough to hold the multitudes who came to hear him. Many a time in the open fields he preached with more than sixty thousand people gathered round him. Fearlessly rebuking the vices of all ranks in society, high and low, rich and poor, many were conscience-stricken under his searching words and came to him, as the like sort came to John the Baptist, freely confessing their sins.

The Preaching Friars soon passed over into England with which we are now more immediately concerned, — the Dominicans, a party of thirteen, arriving in 1220, and the Franciscans, nine in number, in 1224. So completely did they revolutionize the mode of popular address and make their way to the heart of the people that within the space of thirty years the nine Franciscans had multiplied to 1242 and were possessed of forty-nine convents in various parts of the country. In England, as on the continent, the Church had stood coldly aloof from the mass of the people, a favorite illustration with churchmen being that the clergy and laity were as distinct elements as wine and water. The Preaching Friars changed all that. Getting right in among the people whom the Church had so long neglected, they adopted a style of address more suited to their audiences, appealing as it did more directly to the feelings, being more popular and more dramatic. The indolent, lifeless secular clergy resented the intrusion of these new-comers whom they regarded as mere fanatics and troublesome innovators. The charges, however, which they brought against the Friars tend rather to exalt them in our opinion than otherwise. They accused them of studying eloquence and the art of rhetoric in the composition of their sermons; of transgressing the precept of the Apostle who laid it down that preaching was not to be with wisdom of words; of making their addresses agreeable to the people; and finally they said that by mixing with the people as they did, they dragged down the dignity of the clerical office. Better be select and genteel, thought they, even though you die of gentility.

One significant fact about this thirteenth century movement is that while aiming at what some would call mere popular preaching it allied itself with an enlightened love of learning. The scientific speculative spirit of that time, so far as it was imbued with religious feeling, was powerfully influenced by leading Franciscans and Dominicans. As in the first century the greatest missionary, the Apostle Paul, was also the greatest theologian, so in the thirteenth century the most effective teachers of the people were the most ardent metaphysicians and theologians. Among them we find the great schoolmen of the continent — Albertus Magnus, Bonaventura and Thomas Aquinas; also the great English schoolmen — Alexander of Hales, John Duns Scotus and Roger Bacon. The Franciscans had true poets among them. Thomas of Celano was the author of the terrible, sublime hymn, *Dies Irae;* and Jacopone, the greatest poet of the Franciscan school, endowed with true poetic genius and penetrated with the fire of creative passion, composed the celebrated *Stabat Mater.* Then, too, when we visit the memorable monastery of San Marco in Florence we cannot forget that in later years Fra Angelico, the gentle painter whose atmosphere seemed to be innocence, holiness, and purity, was a Dominican, as was also Savonarola, the great Florentine preacher of righteousness to an age of dissolute worldliness.

The late Mr. Brewer, a scholar deeply versed in the knowledge of original sources of English history earned our gratitude by bringing to light the remarkable series of documents published under the title of *Monumenta Franciscana.* In an introduction to that work he asks: "Is it not remarkable that the Friars, the most ardent upholders of scholastic theology, were precisely the men who constituted the most popular preachers of the age? that their sermons are far from being dry expositions of scholastic philosophy? that instead of being appeals to the reason against authority, they contain the most direct appeals to the imagination and the feelings of the people to whom they were addressed?" It is certainly a noteworthy fact for all time and for every generation of preachers that in the case of the Friars we have the most effective popular preaching of the thirteenth century associated with the best learning to which the human mind had attained in that century. The combination must ever be maintained. Mere popular appeals are apt in time to become shallow and evanescent; on the other hand, mere scholarship without broad popular sympathies becomes dry and powerless.

The combination of the two is the ideal for every preacher to aim at in his work. The truest simplicity, the most effective putting of the revelations of God may best be associated with the most solid learning attainable by man.

I am not giving you a history of the Friars; if I were I should have to admit that the Franciscan and Dominican orders, like the older monastic orders before them, became corrupted by the very wealth they professed at the outset to abjure. They fell from their high estate, the gold became dim, the most fine gold changed. We cannot dwell on the utter decay of their ideal, or speak of the fetters of stupid servitude which in a later period of their history they imposed on the freedom of thought and science. We can only mourn over it. It has been well said that, had not ambition corrupted them, they might have revolutionized society, and been the precursors of a far gentler and more spiritual Reformation than that of the sixteenth century. But, the salt having lost its savor, how could it preserve the world?

But though the ardor of popular sympathy displayed by the Friars at first died down under the corrupting influence of wealth and sensual indulgence; and though their scholastic philosophy dwindled at last into mere meaningless and wearisome subtleties, falling by the weight of its own dialectic, they were not without great and lasting influence. Taking their best days, that is, the first twenty-five years of their history, we can see how they form a link between modern and mediæval times. The unreservedness with which as Schoolmen they ranged through every region of metaphysics and divinity led in turn to equal freedom of discussion, equal unreservedness on political lines of thought. Paradoxical as it may seem, it is nevertheless true that the Dominican and Franciscan orders, established for the purpose of strengthening the Papacy, prepared the way in no slight degree for that Reformation which shattered the Papacy. With truth it may be said that even John Wickliffe himself, the Morning Star of the Reformation, as he has been called, is the genuine descendant of the Friars Preachers, turning their wisdom against themselves, and carrying out the principles he had learnt from them to their legitimate conclusions, both ecclesiastical and political. The continuity of history may sometimes be traced along the most unexpected lines.

The preaching of the Friars during the time they were most active and zealous not only produced its own direct effect on the popular mind, but, by way of rivalry, it had the effect of stirring up the bishops and clergy themselves. The Synod of Oxford of 1223 enjoined the clergy "not to be dumb dogs, but with salutary bark to drive away the disease of spiritual wolves from the flock." The Bishop of Coventry required all his clergy to address their people assembled on the Lord's day, or other festivals, in certain words which constituted a rhetorical sermon on the seven deadly sins. The Bishop of Lincoln gave directions to his clergy to preach on Sundays, and gave them the heads of their teaching; and the Bishop of Exeter drew up a similar book for his diocese of which he required every parish to have a copy under penalty of a fine. Canon X, of the Provincial Synod of Lambeth of 1281 A. D., gives us some insight into the sort of teaching prevailing in the Church itself, half a century later than the coming of the Friars. The preamble first speaks of the ignorance of priests and the consequent debasement of the people. For the remedy of such mischiefs, the Canon goes on to say: "We ordain that every priest who presides over a people do four times a year, that is, once in each quarter of the year, on one or more festival days, either by himself or by another, expound to the people in popular language, without any fanciful subtleties the fourteen Articles of Faith, the Ten Commandments of the Lord, the two Evangelical precepts of Charity, the seven works of Mercy, the seven deadly sins with their progeny, the seven principal virtues, and the seven sacraments of Grace."

It is during this period of the Church's history we come upon two or three manuscript specimens of certain Metrical Homilies, which took the place of sermons, and which there is reason to believe were extensively used in the churches, especially in the northern counties. They are interesting as giving the English popular speech of five or six centuries ago; as among the earliest literary efforts of the period immediately preceding that of Chaucer; as illustrating the religious life and habits of a time long gone by; and as being the only remains extant of mediæval popular preaching in the fourteenth century. As respects the substance of these Homilies they consist of portions of Scripture selected from the Gospels. The homilist first goes over the narrative with such reflections as may best convey the practical lesson to his hearers, and then enforces some point of doctrine or practice by a "narracio," that is, a story taken from the Gospels themselves, or from ecclesiastical legends, or the popular tales of the day. Their peculiarity lies, of course, in their being in metrical form, though this was not altogether a new departure, since metrical versions of Scripture had been known in England from the time of Caedmon in the seventh century onwards. While there is much in these Homilies which is coarse and foolish there is much also of sound gospel truth and wholesome moral teaching. They contain faithful, pointed rebukes of evildoers without respect of persons, and earnest calls to righteousness of life; while of the grace, condescension and saving power of our Lord, and of the need of faith in Him and repentance toward God, the various writers of the Homilies speak strongly, frequently and clearly.

The preaching of the Friars was followed by the zealous propaganda of John Wickliffe and his successors; who, while working on much the same lines as the Friars, set forth a more scriptural and evangelical faith. This Lollard movement was instinct with life. As preachers they went forth through the realm from county to county, and from town to town; preaching from day to day, not only in churches and churchyards, but also in open market-place and public thoroughfare. The life thus created, under the blessing of heaven never really died out; and it may be safely maintained that without the Lollards of the fourteenth century the Reformation of the sixteenth would not have been possible. Long after Wickliffe himself had passed away, as John Foxe tells us, "there were secret multitudes who tasted and followed the sweetness of God's Holy Word, and whose fervent zeal may appear by their sitting up all night in reading and hearing." The fruit of the labors of those godly, self-denying preachers was to be seen in after days in what is ever the true preacher's highest reward — in the "earnest seekings, the busy zeal, the watchings, the sweet assemblies, the love and concord, and the godly living" of those who heard them.

II

JOHN COLET AND THE PREACHERS OF THE REFORMATION

LECTURE II

JOHN COLET AND THE PREACHERS OF THE REFORMATION

IN the lecture of yesterday I asked you to review with me the influence exerted by the preaching of the Friars — Franciscan and Dominican, and by the earnest propaganda of Wickliffe and the Preachers he sent forth. This brings us to the border-land of the Reformation time in England. Before we quite pass within that time and onward to the Puritan period which followed, there is one man who stood midway between the old time and the new — John Colet the Oxford Reformer — whose work and influence deserve our careful attention.

The effect upon Europe of the taking of Constantinople by the Turks in 1453, has often been pointed out. Dark were the prophecies and dire the forebodings which followed that event, and which there was much in the previous history of the Moslem to justify. To the men of that time it seemed as if the end of the world had come, or at least, that the death-knell of civilization had sounded. Yet, strangely enough, that which was feared would be the destruction of learning proved to be its revival. For, fleeing before the ruthless Turk, scholars of great reputation migrated from the East to the West, bringing their manuscripts with them. Then, too, as God so willed it—for it is He who determines the time when new and powerful forces shall enter into the life of nations—just then came the invention of the printing press, bringing within the reach of the many the great works of literature once only accessible to the few. In this way Italy became once more the seat of learning; and the city of Florence especially, under the patronage of a De Medici, drew to itself the younger and more enthusiastic spirits of the new time now dawning. Among these was John Colet, an Oxford student, the son of a wealthy London merchant, and the friend of Erasmus and Sir Thomas More.

He seems to have left Oxford about 1493, and travelled to Italy at a time when in Rome the crimes of Pope Alexander VI. and the Borgias were the scandal of Europe on the one side; and when in Florence the powerful preaching of Savonarola set all men thinking of the evil of the times on the other. We have now no means of knowing how the change was brought about while he was abroad, but we do know that John Colet, who while he was at Oxford had "devoured Cicero" and diligently read Plato and Plotinus, now "gave himself up entirely to the study of the Holy Scriptures." Erasmus, who tells us this, tells us also that alongside this main pursuit he paid diligent attention to such chronicles and English classics as he could lay hold of, with the object of mastering their style, and so preparing himself for the great work of preaching the Gospel in England. After being abroad some three years he returned to Oxford in 1496, and though not in Orders and without a doctor's degree, he astonished the University circles by announcing a free course of lectures on St. Paul's Epistles.

In those days a venture like this was new, required courage and created a stir. Doctors and abbots, men of all ranks and titles, were seen mingling with the students in the lecture hall; and having come once they came again and again, "bringing their note-books with them." The venture was entirely successful and there were various reasons why it should be. First of all the lecturer was endowed with that clear and vigorous mode of speech which always tells. In one of his letters Erasmus says to Colet: "You say what you mean, and mean what you say. Your words have birth in your heart, not on your lips. They follow your thoughts instead of your thoughts being shaped by them. You have the happy art of expressing with ease what others can hardly express with the greatest labor." The toil of mastering the English style from the English classics had gone first, and this facility which seemed so natural and so easy was the outcome of the toil. But while from this letter of Erasmus we learn one of the secrets of Colet's success, it was not the only one. For, for the first time he made the Bible to these men a living book. Taking the Epistle to the Romans and showing the logical sequence of thought, the connection of part with part, he made them feel the spirit of the whole; so that they were conscious not merely of being in contact with the Epistle, but still more of being in contact with the man who wrote it. More after the manner of the nineteenth century than the fifteenth, he brought out the personal traits of the apostle's writings, — his "vehemence of speaking," which did not give him time to perfect his sentences; the rare prudence and tact with which he balanced his words to meet the needs of the different classes addressed; his "modesty," "toleration," self-denial and consideration for others; and the reality of application there was in many of his sayings to the circumstances and needs of the time. He stepped aside, too, from the old time-worn ruts of those who furbished up authorities and illustrations merely from the Church fathers. He sought these in the broad fields of the best literature and from the scholars of his own time. The men who listened to him felt that he made the Bible to be altogether a new thing to them, a living force entering into the current of their life.

After carrying on this work from 1496 to 1505 Colet was made Dean of St. Paul's, and the sphere of his influence was thus transferred from Oxford to London. By this change his work was made to tell more directly upon the people at large, for in the same earnest spirit that work was still continued. The chief citizens of London filled the places round his desk hitherto filled by University men. While there was a change of place there was no change of purpose, or of method either. The only change there was lay in the fact that he now seemed drawn rather to the Gospels than to the Epistles. The place in his mind hitherto filled by Paul was now yielded more completely to the Person and teachings of Christ. But his method was the same, for his discourses were not upon isolated texts, but continuous expositions of the facts of the Saviour's life and of the substance of His teaching. That which had made the Bible a new and fascinating book to the men of literature in Oxford, made it a new and fascinating book for the men of business in London also.

Is there not in these facts a certain suggestiveness for ourselves? Colet's method of so dealing with the Scriptures as to make them living books to the men of his time, bringing out the richness and fulness of their teaching, starts again the question, often started before, as to the desirability or otherwise of continuous expository preaching. One can only say that it depends how a man does it as to whether it is desirable or not. It may be made a refuge for idleness, the man flitting over many things because he has not thought out one thing; or, it may be the outcome of the best work a man can do. It has been objected that exposition of continuous sort tends to unutterable tedium and weariness, and men will point you to a folio volume of Arthur Hildersam's, for example, containing a hundred and eight lectures on the fourth chapter of John's Gospel, and to another folio of his containing a hundred and fifty-two lectures on the nineteen verses of the 51st Psalm; and they will tell you that Joseph Caryl began his Exposition of Job with eight hundred hearers and ended with only eight, the patience of his audience not being equal to that of the patriarch on whose experiences he descanted so long. The late Mr. Spurgeon said that he never dared enter upon a continuous course of teaching, that brethren of extraordinary research and profound learning might do it, but he could not, for he was obliged to owe a great deal of his strength to variety rather than profundity. It seemed to him that to go through a long epistle must require a great deal of genius in the preacher, and demand a world of patience on the part of the hearers. He never could preach, he said, till he met with a text that gripped him by the hand; that when a text gets a hold of us, we may be sure that we have a hold of it and may safely deliver our souls upon it. For his part, he must take the text that God sent him and he knows which it is by these signs, that it grew before his eye like the fabled seed which developed into a tree while the observer watched it; that it charmed and fascinated him or weighed him to his knees, loading him with the burden of the Lord. He must wait for that elect word, he said, even if he had to wait till within an hour of the service.

Well, that is one side of the question, no doubt, but there is another side. I am convinced, for my own part, that the great want of many Christian people in our time is a more thorough and systematic knowledge of the Word of God. They need it for spiritual enlightenment and also for Christian steadfastness. I have spoken with people who have listened to sermons all their lives and nothing surprises me more than to hear them relate their spiritual perplexities. They are often such as never would have arisen had they read their Bibles more intelligently. A man who has grasped the central idea of a book, mastered its main principles, must of necessity see its details in a much clearer light than the man who has not. I am not contending for an elaborate and exhaustive treatment of every line of every verse like that which John Owen has given in his Exposition of the Epistle to the Hebrews. Life is not long enough, and things move too fast nowadays for that. But even the Epistle to the Hebrews, as Dr. Dale has shown us, may become instinct with life, when a living man takes it in hand and holds it up to the light. His exposition of that Epistle, as his biographer tells us, was the work of a busy man, and for that very reason comes close to practical life and its daily needs. The truths taught in the Epistle are translated into the speech of our own day; there is nothing about it merely academic and no remoteness in the teaching. I venture to think that people of average intelligence who paid anything like fair attention to that exposition would feel at the end that not only had light been shed on the Epistle itself, but also on the whole of their Bible such as they had never had before. Every man must be a judge for himself and take the gauge of his own powers, but if now and again in the course of a ministry — to say no more — the preacher would give some amount of systematic instruction as to the mind of the Spirit, he would go far to establish his people in the truth, strengthen their shaken faith and revive their spiritual passion. And so far as he himself is concerned he would come to know as never before some of the deepest joys of the Christian student's life. Mr. Spurgeon has told us how a single text may grip, may charm and fascinate you. But a whole book of Scripture may grip you closer and charm and fascinate you even more. By way of illustration let me again refer to Dr. Dale. In 1882 he published a series of Expositions of the Epistle to the Ephesians which he had first given to his own people. Twelve years later, only a few months before his death, writing to a correspondent he says: "If I can lay my hands on a copy of my lectures on the Ephesians this afternoon I shall take the liberty of sending it to you. It is the book of mine that I like best: Paul found me the material, and I had nothing to do but to say over again what he had already said." Yes, but in another letter he shows us that he not only *said* over again what Paul had said but that he also *saw* over again the streaming glory which Paul had seen. Referring to the same epistle and writing to another expositor, he says: "I hope that you had as much delight in working at the Epistle as I had. Some parts of it intoxicated me; whether I was in the body or out of the body I could hardly tell." So, there are joys not of this world to the preacher himself as well as to his people when he digs deep into the rich mine of sacred truth.

Passing from John Colet and his expository methods let us now place ourselves in thought in that Reformation time which he lived not to see but for which he did much to prepare. After the Reformation had become an accomplished fact, and men had time to realize the true state of affairs, it was found that the most urgent need of the nation was that of preachers for the people. For under the Papacy preaching had been made to give place so almost entirely to mere ceremonial and ritual in worship that there were very few who could preach. In 1535 the Archbishop of York said that in all his province, which at that time included the northern part of Lancashire, he did not know of twelve ministers who were able to preach. In many parishes there had been little of any religious teaching of Scriptural sort for generations. The President of the Council of the North informed the Privy Council that there were churches and churches where there had literally never been a sermon for years. The prophet had given place to the priest, and always when that is the case, the people's ignorance becomes the nation's danger. It was felt that something must be done, and done at once, and the remedy which seemed to lie nearest to hand was to order the preachers in the Cathedral churches to divide themselves in the dioceses where they dwelt, and travel from place to place preaching the Word to the people. Parts of the province of Canterbury were quite as benighted as some of those in the province of York. There, too, there were parishes in the churches of which a sermon had not been heard for years. There were some who thought it to be a great step in advance when it was laid down by authority of the State that a sermon must be preached in each church once every quarter. While on the other hand there were others who replied with disappointment that four sermons in a year, and only four, were as little likely to make perfect men in Christ Jesus as four strokes of an axe were to fell a mighty oak, or as four showers of an hour long were to moisten the hard dry earth and make it fruitful the whole year long.

In Lancashire men were appointed who were

called King's Preachers, whose duty it was to itinerate, preaching the doctrines of the Reformation in the more benighted parts of the country. Foremost among these was John Bradford, who was afterwards one of the martyrs of Queen Mary's time, a man of bold and daring energy who had great power of command over an audience. Filled with the spirit of God and with a passionate love for Christ and the souls of men, wherever he was announced to preach the people crowded round him, their beating hearts responding to his burning words. A contemporary of his who often heard him preach sets him before us in a way which may make him serve as a model in some not unimportant respects. "He was," he says, "in those times a master of speech; but he had learned from his Master not to speak what he could speak, but what his hearers could hear. He knew that clearness of speech was the excellency of speech; and therefore resolved with a good orator to speak beneath himself rather than above his auditory. Otherwise his eloquence was confessedly great, that is, native, masculine, modest, in one word, heavenly. For if you mark him he savors and breathes nothing but heaven; yea, he sparkles, thunders, lightens, pierces the soft, breaks only the stony heart. Whether he were better preacher or scholar, is to me a great question. He was of a most sweet, humble and melting spirit, who (I know not how) will be in a man's bosom ere he be aware, and willingly win him from himself to Christ."

There is one other man of that time, Bradford's colleague in service and afterwards his fellow-sufferer in the fires of martyrdom, Hugh Latimer, who also stands before our minds as a sturdy English preacher, and one of the heroes of the Reformation time. Not many years ago an elm tree shed its autumn leaves over the spot in St. Paul's churchyard where once stood in London city a cross which surmounted the most celebrated pulpit in England. The tree has disappeared, like the structure it was planted to commemorate, but in Hugh Latimer's sermons we can still recall some of the glowing sentences which in the bygone time made the old cathedral walls to echo. Other preachers have excelled him in passion, stirring rhetoric, refinement, and accuracy; but few have proved his equals in broad forceful influence over all classes of people, and his sermons remain as the prose classics of his day. There was a racy freshness, often a strong sense of humor, and always a sturdy vigor about his utterances which in days when the newspaper had not yet appeared and the public meeting was not yet organized, dealt trenchantly with the vices, the follies, and the superstitions of the time. While faithfully proclaiming Bible fact and truth he was vigilant and urgent against all sorts of abuses both in Church and State, in private and in social life. With his homely invective he spares no class, passes by no form of oppression. His sermons were often deficient in method, but as you might see by the faces of the people they always hit the mark and made the target ring. No one reads them now for theological instruction, but they are still fresh and living, which is more than can be said for a good deal of that kind of literature. The lordly bishops of the time who sat in lofty dignity on their cathedral thrones, or indulged the love of ease in stately palaces, leaving other people to do the preaching, must have winced under a passage which is familiar enough, but which will bear repeating. "Who is the most diligentest bishop and prelate in all England, that passeth all the rest in doing his office? I can tell, for I know him who it is — I know him well.

But now I think I see you listening and hearkening that I should name him. There is one that passeth all others and is the most diligent prelate and preacher in all England. And will you know who it is? I will tell you — it is the devil. He is the most diligent preacher of all others. He is never out of his diocese, he is never from his cure; ye shall never find him unoccupied; he is ever in his parish; he keepeth residence at all times; ye shall never find him out of the way; call for him when you will, he is ever at home; he is ever at his plough; no lording nor loitering can hinder him — you will never find him idle, I warrant you. And his office is to hinder religion, to maintain superstition, to set up idolatry. When the devil is resident and hath his plough going, then away with books and up with candles; away with Bibles and up with beads; away with the light of the Gospel and up with the light of candles, yea, at noonday. . . . Down with Christ's cross and up with purgatory pickpurse — the Popish purgatory, I mean.... Up with man's traditions and his laws, down with God's traditions and His most holy Word; down with the old honor due to God, and up with the new god's honors."

That was living talk straight from the soul of a living man, and if you could always get these two things together, no one would ever dream of saying that the time will come when the pulpit will be superseded by the press. For the great work of the Church of God in the world a living man must always be more than a printed sheet.

Hugh Latimer was what other prophets of God have been — both martyr and prophet, and with his martyrdom came the downfall of Protestantism for a while. During the five years Queen Mary sat on the English throne there is nothing to be said about the preacher or his vocation, for he was supplanted by the priest and hunted from one hiding place to another. The priests of the Romish Baal were in the high places of the land, and the prophets of the Lord were either burning at the stake or wearing out their lives in exile. The history of those five years is stained with the blood of brave and saintly men and women; but all noble self-sacrifice for truth and right leaves a blessing behind. Those years have made it impossible that ever such years should come again. They have left memories behind them which Rome with all her craft and cunning will never be able to wipe away; and they explain why it was that when they came to an end at last the wheel swung full cycle round and Protestantism was once more the religion of the realm.

Out of a restored Protestantism came that Puritanism which is Protestantism in its more fully developed form. And now that we have reached this point, it may be well before proceeding to speak of the preachers of Puritan times, to define what we mean by Puritanism and to try to reduce to something like mental order the religious and ecclesiastical phenomena of the Elizabethan Church. Speaking generally it may be safely said that in the beginning of Elizabeth's reign that Church, so far as its leaders were concerned, was not only Protestant but Puritan and Calvinistic. The Roman Catholic bishops — all but one who faced about — had disappeared; and the Anglican divines who took their places were all of them stanch Protestants. During the troubles of the Marian time the latter were living as exiles for their faith in Frankfort, Strasburg, Geneva, Zurich and elsewhere, where they were hospitably received by the Foreign Protestants, between whom and themselves warm friendships still continued to subsist even after the return of the exiles, as the Zurich Letters remain to testify. If these men could have had their way they would have set up forms of worship not far removed from those of continental Protestantism. Bishop Jewell may be taken as a thoroughly representative man of the earlier time, and, writing to his friend Bullinger at Zurich in 1566, speaking of the vestments and the ceremonies he plainly says: "I wish that all, even the slightest vestiges of popery, might be removed from our churches, and above all from our minds. But the Queen is unable to endure the least alteration in matters of religion." In a still earlier letter to Peter Martyr he had spoken even more contemptuously of the attempt some were making to set up ceremonial display in the worship of God. He says: "The scenic apparatus of Divine worship is now under agitation; and those very things which you and I have so often laughed at are now seriously and solemnly entertained by certain persons, as if the Christian religion could not exist without something tawdry." Clearly this Anglican bishop was a Puritan of the Puritans, so far as the externals of worship were concerned. Even in Convocation, in 1563, when a resolution was brought forward to put away the vestments and ceremonies to which the Puritans objected, there was actually among those present a majority in its favor, and it was only when proxies were called for that it was lost by one vote. It was the steadfast resistance of the Queen alone, who liked pomp and ceremony in church as she did elsewhere, that prevented Protestantism taking a more puritanical form than it did in the earlier years of its history. Even to the end of her reign, so far as doctrine was concerned, the Anglican Church remained strongly Calvinistic. As late as 1595, one William Barret — "a bold, corrupt and unlearned young fellow," as the Heads of Colleges at Cambridge described him — in a sermon before the University expressed himself unfavorably against Calvin's doctrine of predestination. The authorities of the University were unanimous in their condemnation of the preacher. And though Archbishop Whitgift is justly regarded as the bitter enemy of the Puritans, he showed himself as resolute a Calvinist in doctrine as any Puritan in the land. He at once sent down to Cambridge nine propositions, commonly called the Lambeth Articles, the first of which declared that "God from eternity has predestinated some persons to life, and reprobated others to death;" the third affirmed that "the number of the predestinated is fixed and cannot be lessened or increased;" and the ninth and last proposition stands absolutely alone in its appalling simplicity, for it goes so far as to say: "It is not in the will and power of every man to be saved." Clearly, so far as predestination is concerned no Puritan could go beyond the doctrinal position of this archbishop who persecuted the Puritans.

Yet while the doctrines of Calvin were accepted by the Anglican Church right on to the end of the reign of Elizabeth they were never really at home in the Anglican system. They were a foreign element brought in with the first great impulse of Protestantism and have never been assimilated. To this day Evangelical Churchmen have never been able to make the Articles of the Prayer Book harmonize with the Rubrics of the Prayer Book. Sooner or later it was inevitable that Puritan and Anglican should part company, for they were not agreed in their conception of the standard of final authority in religion. The Puritans fell back upon Scripture and Scripture alone. The Anglican, while accepting Scripture as the original depository of Christian truth, acknowledged ecclesiastical tradition as its legitimate expositor. He appealed less to personal experience than to the general judgment of antiquity. Accepting Scripture and tradition as joint witnesses and authorities in matters of faith, the idea of the Church came to be that of an external institution with an elaborate system of means for connecting heaven and earth. The Thirty-Nine Articles were still retained in the Prayer Book, but in the early days of James I. they were more and more left out of the sermon until it was true, as Lord Chatham said, that the Church had a Calvinistic creed, an Arminian clergy, and a Popish liturgy.

The Puritan discarded tradition and would have nothing to do with a priestly hierarchy. He boldly claimed to be able to draw nigh to God through Christ for himself; maintained that separate communities of believing men were true churches of Christ resting on a divine foundation. The Puritan minister held that his authority came direct from the Lord and was valid as recognized by believing men in whom dwelt the Spirit of God; and believing that faith cometh by hearing not by church ceremonies, and that salvation means personal submission of heart and life to Christ, he felt himself under solemn obligation to labor unceasingly to bring men to God. The Puritan layman on his part also felt that he must bring his own understanding into patient and thoughtful exercise in the study of Scripture, and not let the Church do his thinking for him. As a natural consequence the search after truth carried on thus under a high sense of personal responsibility to God issued in the formation of habits of mental independence, profound seriousness, and manly self-reliance. Whatever may be said as to the æsthetic or non-æsthetic side of Puritanism — and much more has been said than is borne out by the facts of history — Puritan principles gave to Puritan men an indomitable love of freedom, high courage, stern integrity, and unbending faithfulness to the deepest convictions of the soul. The men who at the beginning of Elizabeth's reign seemed to be substantially one, at the end of half a century, by the sheer force of the idea of the Church they had severally accepted, found themselves wide asunder. They were asunder politically as well as ecclesiastically. For under the Stuarts the Anglo-Catholic, believing in authority, took sides with absolutism in political government, and in his blindness proclaimed the divine right of kings to govern wrong. On the other hand the Puritan, as we might expect, cast in his lot with the political party contending for freedom and constitutional government. He became the effective force of that party; and when the two systems came at last, as they did, to open conflict in the Great Civil War of the seventeenth century, victory was finally declared on the side of Freedom by the great battles of Naseby and Marston Moor. It will be seen from this rapid summary that a process of change was going forward; that therefore what was true of church parties at one period was only partially true ten or twenty years later; and that it would be correct to describe as Puritan preachers men who were still strongly attached to the Anglican Church.

At the latter end of Elizabeth's reign it was urgently felt that there was need of more and more regular religious instruction among the people; and in Convocation "order was taken" in the matter of preaching. Every licensed preacher was to give twelve sermons every year in the diocese where his benefice lay; and six or seven preachers were appointed to minister "by course" in parishes where no licensed preacher was. What took place in Manchester may perhaps be taken as typical of what was done elsewhere. There the bishop of the diocese set up a public exercise to be held on the second Thursday in every month; and nominated certain grave, godly, and learned ministers to preach in rotation. And as the clergy needed teaching almost as much as the people, all parsons, vicars, curates, readers, and schoolmasters within the deanery were commanded to be present. Further they were to be ready in the afternoon to be more privately conferred with, examined, instructed, and directed, under pain of censure.

Subsequently the lords of the Council ordered the farther enlargement of these exercises and their extension to other parts of the diocese. In accordance with this direction similar exercises were established in several large towns of the county, usually once a month on the market day. It is evident from some of the facts which have come down to us that these preachings or "prophesyings" met a want among the more earnest-minded of the people. On the Thursday of the monthly exercise in Manchester many of the inhabitants of the neighboring towns, long before the commencement of the service, crowded the Collegiate Church, which must have presented a somewhat animated appearance. The five moderators — the five nominated grave, godly, and learned ministers, were there in grave and sober apparel, for in spite of all orders to the contrary the surplice was scarcely ever worn by the Puritan clergy of Lancashire. The bishop also was frequently present in his robes, for, Puritan as he was, he usually distinguished himself from his clergy by wearing his canonicals. Now and then the Earl of Derby attended in some state with a considerable retinue, and the Puritan magistrates generally occupied a conspicuous place in the church. As to the discourses of the first five of the preachers, we have not much information, but a contemporary tells us of one William Bourne, who succeeded the last of the five, that he "seldom varied the manner of his preaching, which after explication of the text, was doctrine proof of it from Scripture, by reasoning and answering more and more objections; and then the uses, first, of information, secondly, of confutation of popery, thirdly, of reprehension, fourthly, of examination, fifthly, of exhortation, and lastly of consolation."

To show you, however, that all the preachers of that time were not quite so stereotyped in method, let me, by way of concluding this lecture, introduce you to "that eloquent divine of famous memory Thomas Playfere," who was Lady Margaret Professor of Divinity at Cambridge in Queen Elizabeth's time, and afterwards court preacher to King James. In a sermon entitled "The Pathway to Perfection" based on Philippians iii. 14, he begins by saying that as Solomon went up six steps to come to his great throne of ivory, so must we ascend six degrees to come to this high top of perfection. He therefore proceeds to divide his text into six parts. On that part which deals with the Apostle's forgetting those things which are behind, Playfere says: "He that remembers his virtues hath no virtues to remember, seeing he wants humility, which is the mother virtue of all virtues. For this is the difference between the godly and the wicked: both remember virtues, but the godly remember other men's virtues, the wicked remember their own. Wherefore though thou have conquered kingdoms yet crake not of it as Sennacherib did: though thou hast built Babel yet brag not of it as Nebuchadnezzar did; though thou hast rich treasures yet show them not as Hezekiah did; though thou hast slain a thousand Philistines yet glory not in it as Samson did; though thou give alms yet blow not a trumpet; though thou fast twice a week yet make no words of it, (remember it not but) Forget that which is behind."

On the prize of the high calling mentioned in the text he pours out his soul in rapture thus: "O happy, happy man art thou, and thrice happy man art thou! For when we shall see God, we shall see, and what shall we see? That which no mortal eye hath seen that we shall see. We shall see our own as sitting and shining at the right hand of the throne of Majesty. We shall see all our dear friends which we have not seen this many a day, embracing us and welcoming us into Christ's kingdom. We shall see all the noble army of martyrs, of apostles, of prophets, of patriarchs day and night singing out the praises of the Lord. We shall see all the invincible host of angels, of archangels, of principalities, of dominions reverently attending upon the King of Glory. We shall see the King himself disparkling and displaying those beams of beauty which are the Heavens' wonder and all the angels' bliss."

In a sermon entitled "Heart's Delight" on the text "Delight thyself in the Lord," he thus exclaims: "Nay, I cannot hold my heart for my joy; yea, I cannot hold my joy for my heart; to think that He which is my Lord is become my Father, and so that He which was offended with me for my sin's sake, is now reconciled to me for His Son's sake. To think that the High Majesty of God will one day raise me out of the dust, and so that I who am now a poor worm upon earth shall hereafter be a glorious saint in heaven. This, this makes me delight myself in the Lord, saying, O Thou that art the delight of my delight, the life of my life, the soul of my soul, I delight myself in Thee, I live only for Thee, I offer myself unto Thee, wholly to Thee wholly, one to Thee one, only to Thee only. For suppose now, as St. John speaketh, the whole world were full of books, and all the creatures in the world were writers, and all the grass piles upon the earth were pens, and all the waters in the sea were ink; yet I assure you faithfully all these books, all these writers, all these pens, all this ink would not be sufficient to describe the very least part, either of the goodness of the Lord in himself, or of the lovingkindness of the Lord towards thee."

III

THE CAMBRIDGE PURITANS

LECTURE III

THE CAMBRIDGE PURITANS

IN this lecture I will ask you to go back with me to the earlier years of the Puritan movement, of which I have already spoken, that I may introduce to you some of the preachers who were the makers of Puritanism. The men who were the leaders in that movement, who gave it its distinctive character, were almost all of them University men, and for the most part Cambridge men. In the second half of the sixteenth century Cambridge was described as "a nest of Puritans." Emmanuel is usually regarded as the one distinctively Puritan College of that University; but it should be noted that, twenty years before Emmanuel was founded, Christ's College led the way, being strongly Protestant almost as soon as Protestantism was re-established under Elizabeth. A young man named Laurence Chaderton, coming up to Cambridge from one of the old Roman Catholic families of Lancashire and entering at Christ's in 1564, found himself at once in the midst of men who had zealously embraced the doctrines of the Reformation. It was a new world to him and opened up new ways of thinking; and, as one who knew him well tells us, he went through severe mental struggle; deliberately examined the points in dispute between the adherents of the new faith and the old, and with many and earnest prayers decided in favor of the Reformers. The result came, as he says, from various sources — study of the Bible, the conversation of his fellows, and that mental agitation and movement which men look upon as a "call" from God. His Roman Catholic father, away up in Lancashire, heard with consternation the news of this change of faith on the part of his son, and wrote at once to say that if he would renounce the new sect he had joined, he would care for him as an indulgent father; "otherwise," said he, "I enclose in this letter a shilling to buy a wallet with. Go and beg for your living. Farewell!" Undaunted by difficulty, however, Chaderton held on his way, gained a fellowship and became a successful tutor at Christ's.

But it is in this man as a preacher we are specially interested, and it was in this work he exercised his most memorable influence.

Before his time preaching had become a rarity in the University, but now, for nearly fifty years, as afternoon lecturer at St. Clement's Church, he gathered large congregations both from the town and the university. With natural gifts, acquired attainments, and a wonderful zeal for winning men, Chaderton obtained great influence in the pulpit. He seems to have had pre-eminent qualifications for the work. In the investigation of Scripture he displayed great acuteness of mind and keen spiritual insight; and he had the not too common faculty of being able to seize upon and forcibly present the main aspects of a subject. As a speaker his style was eminent for purity, lucidity, manliness, and sincerity; and it was specially noted that when in prayer, he became affected with such ardor himself as not only to fire the souls of his hearers, but to carry and raise them with him to heaven. Possessed of a voice clear and pleasing and of much flexibility; with great dignity of manner, and that propriety of action which Cicero has called "the eloquence of the body," he seems to have been an almost ideal preacher. But while many things contributed to his success, the main power of the man was spiritual;

and it was a fine tribute to his influence that when late in life he thought of resigning his lectureship, he received no fewer than forty letters from as many Christian ministers urging him to continue, if he could, alleging that they themselves, every one of them, while they were at the university had been brought to a knowledge of the truth under his ministry.

Besides the forty ministers who thus wrote letters of entreaty to Laurence Chaderton, two other preachers, in whom we are interested, came under his influence. One of these was his own brother-in-law, Ezekiel Culverwell, who, on leaving the university, went to be minister at Groton Manor near Sudbury. Here he had a memorable hearer in his congregation, a young man of eighteen, John Winthrop afterwards better known to the world as Governor Winthrop. The coming of Culverwell proved to be to this hearer of his an important event in his spiritual history, for now, as he tells us, the Word came home to him with *power*, he having found only *light* before. "Now came I," says he, "to some peace and comfort in God and in His ways; loved a Christian and the very ground on which he trod; honoured a faithful minister in my heart, and could have kissed his feet."

The other man besides Culverwell, both intellectually and spiritually influenced by Chaderton was William Perkins, a Puritan preacher of more than ordinary spiritual power. John Cotton of Boston came under his influence and fought hard against it at first, from a fear that if he became a godly man it would spoil him for being a learned man. But God's truth as ministered by William Perkins proved to be stronger than John Cotton's wilfulness, and eventually he left the university both godly and learned to do a great work for God in both Bostons, that of the Old Country and that of the New. Then again, John Robinson, of Pilgrim Father fame, was among the undergraduates who listened to the burning words of William Perkins in the University Church. He, too, carried this influence with him through life. He quotes this man again and again in his works and also reprinted one of his books at William Brewster's press for the benefit of his own people in the Leyden church. I mention these facts in passing because they show us who are preachers that we do not always know in our own life-time what we are doing when faithfully working for God. The man to whom you pass the torch of heaven's light hands it on to another and he again to others after him. Laurence Chaderton, for example, who never set foot on your shores, is yet living in the religious life of America to-day. For, as we have seen, he imparted his own spirit to Ezekiel Culverwell, who under God begets a diviner life in Governor Winthrop. The same man in another line of influence powerfully sways William Perkins, who, in his turn again, shapes both John Cotton of Boston and John Robinson the honored pastor of the Pilgrim Fathers' church. And thus in a very real sense both these men are living among you still. This is the true Apostolical Succession — the only succession worth caring for.

In the case of a man at once so learned as a scholar, so able as a preacher, and so widely influential as a spiritual force as William Perkins, the preacher of to-day may well be interested in knowing what were his methods and what his ideals. Phineas Fletcher the poet, author of "The Purple Island," speaks of him thirty years later as "our wonder though long dead;"

and quaint Thomas Fuller pays him the compliment of saying that "his sermons were not so plain but that the piously learned did admire them, nor so learned but that the plain did understand them." Theology, Perkins described as "the science of living blessedly for ever;" and he discussed its main doctrines in such sort as to abandon abstruse and unprofitable topics, and with such solemn and impassioned discourse as to win the ear of the most varied audience, method and fervor presenting themselves in rare combination.

As to his ideals — what the Christian preacher should strive to be and to aim at, he has told us himself in certain addresses which he delivered publicly in the university and which were taken down and preserved for us by his loving disciple William Crashaw. I shall help you, I think, and furnish true inspiration, if I briefly summarize for you the main points of addresses given by a master-workman to certain university divinity students and preachers now three hundred years ago. The subject of these addresses was "The Calling of the Ministry, describing the Duties and Dignities of that Calling." Speaking within the bounds of the university, Perkins begins by saying: Most of us in this place are either prophets or the sons of prophets. If we are prophets we are God's messengers and must preach God's Word *as* God's Word and deliver it as we received it. For as many men mar a good tale in the telling, so we must see to it lest we take away the power and majesty of God's Word in the manner of delivering it. Every true minister is a double interpreter — God's interpreter to the people by preaching to them from God, and the people's interpreter to God, laying open their wants, confessing their sins, craving pardon and forgiveness for, and in their names giving thanks for mercies received, thus so offering up their spiritual sacrifices to God. So that every one who either is, or intends to be a minister needs that tongue of the learned of which Isaiah speaks, by which he may be able to speak a word in season to him that is weary. To be able to speak with this tongue the minister must first be furnished with human learning, next with divine knowledge, and besides these with that inward learning taught by the Spirit of God. The two first he must learn from men, the third from God: a true minister must be inwardly taught by the spiritual schoolmaster, the Holy Ghost. He must not only have the knowledge of divine things flowing in his brain, but engraven in his heart and printed in his soul by the spiritual finger of God. After all his own study, meditation, conference, commentaries, after all human helps he must pray with the Psalmist, 'Open thou mine eyes that I may see the wonders of thy Law.' Then too he must labor for sanctity and holiness of life. A minister is to declare the reconciliation betwixt God and man, and is he himself not reconciled? Dare he present another man to God's mercy for pardon and never yet presented himself? Can he commend the state of grace to another, and never felt the sweetness thereof in his own soul? Dare he come to preach sanctification with polluted lips and out of an unsanctified heart? Let all true ministers of God first be God's interpreters to their own consciences, and their own souls' interpreters to God, then shall they know more perfectly how to discharge the office of true interpreters betwixt God and His people. And while they must privately confer, visit admonish and rebuke, yet principally they must *preach*, and that in such good manner and in so diligent measure as they may redeem and win souls — the end they must aim at must be to win souls. Some preach for *fear* of the law, to avoid censure or punishment; some for *fashion's sake*, that they may be like others; some for *ostentation's sake* to win credit and praise; some for *ambition*, to rise in the world: All these forget their commission, which is *to deliver a man from going down to hell.*

In dealing further with the duties and dignities of the ministry Perkins spoke of the making of a prophet as set forth in the vision of Isaiah. At the sight of the Eternal the man of God was humbled to the dust and cried, Woe is me for I am undone! "Yes," says he, "this is God's way. All true ministers, especially such as are deputed to the greatest works in His Church must be first of all stricken with a great fear in consideration of the greatness of their function, yea, into an amazement and astonishment, in the admiration of God's glory and greatness, whose room they occupy and whose message they bring. And the more they are afraid and shrink, so it be under the contemplation of God's majesty and their own weakness the more likely it is that they are truly called of God, and appointed for worthy purposes in His Church." Looking round upon his audience he went on to say: "The use of this, as it is for all ministers, so especially for us who live in the University. We, many of us, are hereafter by God's grace to be framed to the ministry, as some of us already are. Now here we have many occasions to be put up in self-conceit. We see ourselves grow in time, in degrees, in learning, in honor, in name and estimation, and to many of us God gives good portions of His gifts. What are all these but so many baits to allure us to pride and vain opinions of our own worth? But let us remember that our purpose is to save souls and that our weapons in this warfare must not be carnal as pride, vainglory and self-conceit. If therefore we ever look to be made instruments of God's glory in saving souls let us set before our eyes not only the honour but also the danger of our calling and humble ourselves under the mighty hand of God that He may exalt us in due time. Let us be content that God give any occasion or means to pull us down either by outward crosses or inward temptations, and let us rejoice when we are thereby so far cast down that we cry out in the astonishment of our spirits, as the prophet did: 'Woe is me, for I am undone.' Those men do pronounce the most powerful blessings on other men's souls, and speak the best word to other men's consciences, who oftenest say unto themselves, 'Woe is me, for I am undone!'

"The prophet specially exclaimed that he felt himself to be a man of unclean lips — why unclean of lips rather than of heart or hands? Because he was a prophet and his tongue was to be used as a principal instrument of God's glory. Every man is to be tested what he is by his calling rather than by something collateral; therefore the honor or dishonor of a minister, is the use or abuse of his tongue, and his comfort or discomfort is the well using or not using of it. If he use not, or abuse his tongue, the uncleanness of his lips will be the heaviest burden of all. They therefore are greatly deceived who think a minister to discharge sufficiently his duty, though he preach not, if he keep good hospitality, and make peace amongst neighbours and perform other works of charity and good life. For if a minister have not this virtue, he hath none. If he preach not, if he abuse his lips, or if he open them not, he hath no conscience, nor can have any comfort; for that is the principal duty of a minister, though all the other be required to make him complete.

"Still while good words are good, good words are vain where there is no good life. Let not ministers think that their golden words shall do so much good as their leaden lives shall do hurt. It is a vain conceit for men to imagine there is any force in eloquence or human learning to overthrow that sin in others which ruleth and reigneth in themselves. Let the churches take note of this. For it is the glory of a church to have their doctrine powerful and effectual for the winning of souls; therefore it concerneth them to take order, as well that their ministers be godly men as good scholars: and their lives be inoffensive as well as their doctrine sound; or else they will find in woeful experience that they pull down as much with one hand, as they build up with the other. But while this toucheth the churches it more nearly concerns ministers themselves, who must know their case is most fearful of all men's, if they come into God's presence in their profaneness. For as no man is more honorable than a learned and holy minister, so none is more contemptible in this world, none more miserable for that to come than he who by his loose and lewd life doth scandalize his doctrine.

"While sin, even the least sin, nay a very sinfulness of man makes a man afraid of God's presence the way to true courage and boldness before God is to repent daily of sin and labor to grow in true holiness. Wealth nor wit, learning nor authority can do this for thee, but only a good conscience, made good by grace and repentance. Then shalt thou rejoice in God's presence in this world, and delight to think of God, to speak of God, to pray unto Him, to meet Him in His Word and Sacraments, and at the last day shalt thou stand with confidence before the throne of His glory."

On the matter of the touching of the prophet's lips with a burning coal from the altar, he says "This signifies that the apt and sufficient teacher must have a tongue of fire, full of power and force, even like fire to eat up the sins and corruptions of the world. For though it be a worthy gift of God to speak mildly and moderately, so that his speech shall fall like dew upon the grass, yet it is the tongue of fire that beats down sin and works sound grace in the heart. It may be there are some who need the tongue of fire. But it must be fire taken from the altar of God, it must be fire from heaven, his zeal must be a godly and heavenly zeal. He that hath a malicious and contentious tongue hath a tongue of fire, but if a man stand up to preach with this tongue God will never suffer any great work to be done by him in His Church, though his tongue be never so fiery and his speech never so powerful."

The prophet having purged lips heard the voice of the Lord, saying: Whom shall I send, and who will go for us? "We who are in the Universities," Perkins says, "are here admonished to look to ourselves. By God's blessing we are many, and daily grow more and more; let us therefore so furnish ourselves as that when God or His Church shall say Who will go for us? He may find many among us whom He may send to that great work of the ministry.

"Then if He send them they are His servants and if they are His servants they are not their own masters. They may not therefore please themselves, nor serve their own pleasures, nor seek their own credit or profit. If they be God's messengers and servants it follows too that they must not be the servants of men to please or to flatter or satisfy fancies of theirs. It is not for God's servants to be slaves to the persons, or pleasures or humors of men. In all their undertakings they must forthwith call to mind the question Who sent me hither and for whom am I come? Even from and for God, and therefore am I to yield to nothing or aim at anything but what may be both to the will and for the glory of Him who sent me. If ministers be God's servants then let them regard their Master's glory, and be ashamed to do anything either in doctrine or life which may dishonor Him. If, too, they be God's ambassadors, then must they not deliver their own fancies or inventions, but that message they received; and as they received it so must they deliver it. If they do this, if they do their duties faithfully, they may take their pains with joy for they have a master who will reward them; they may speak freely, so it be with discretion, for they have a master who will make it good; they may stand boldly in the face of their enemies for they have a master who will defend them. Every faithful minister may say to himself, I will do my duty and deliver my embassage: He whom I serve and whose I am, He who sent me and for whom I come, will bear me out."

The years when William Perkins's influence was greatest both in the town and in the university — the years from 1590 till his death in 1602 — were the golden age of English Literature. It has been truly said that there are no such ten years either in that or any other literature as the nineties of the sixteenth century, when you can point to an equal number of masterpieces and masters. For taking not the time of writing but of publication as the criterion, we associate these years with the production of Spenser's "Faërie Queene," and the earlier certain plays of Shakespeare; the historical poems of Drayton and Daniel; the satires of Hall, Lodge and Marston; the earliest plays of Ben Jonson, Chapman and Dekker; the Essays of Bacon and the "Ecclesiastical Polity" of Hooker. The mere enumeration of these works may well fill us with wonder. It was an outburst of tropical luxuriance after a time of dearth.

As we might expect, all this affluence of mind told both directly and indirectly upon the pulpit of the time. If it were in our power now to travel over the whole ground other names might be cited in proof that it did, but there are two preachers to whom I may refer who are not unworthy to stand out even in the searching light of that brilliant time. One of these was Henry Smith, known as the silver-tongued preacher, and therefore, as Thomas Fuller says, only one metal below Chrysostom, the golden-mouthed, himself. After a brief time at Cambridge we find him living as a student with a quaint Puritan preacher of the time, Richard Greenham, rector of Dry Drayton in Cambridgeshire, who seems to have thoroughly imbued him with Puritan principles. It was probably through his influence that Smith, from conscientious scruples on the matter of subscription, declined to undertake a pastoral charge, and contented himself with one of those Puritan lectureships, common then and later, which combined opportunities for preaching with more than ordinary freedom for the preacher. Elected in 1587 as Lecturer at St. Clement Danes, London, he quickly rose to great popularity, and came to be spoken of as the "prime preacher of the nation." Wood tells us that he came to be "esteemed the miracle and wonder of his age, for his prodigious memory, and for his fluent, eloquent and practical way of preaching." He was, it may be, all the more welcome to his hearers from the fact that his sermons were almost entirely free from those numerous divisions and subdivisions of his subject, and from those elaborate statements of doctrine in which other preachers of the time indulged. They were free also from that "churchiness" of tone in which later Anglican divines abounded; they were practical, pungent, and interspersed with vivid and luminous character sketches.

His theory of simplicity in preaching will commend itself to you. "There is," said he, "a kind of preachers risen up of late which shroud and cover every rustical and unsavory and childish and absurd sermon under the name of the simple kind of teaching. But indeed to preach simply is not to preach rudely, nor unlearnedly, nor confusedly, but to preach plainly and perspicuously that the simplest man may understand what is taught, as if he did hear his name." And while he has thus a word for the preacher he has one for the hearers too. In a sermon on "The Art of Hearing," he says there are divers ways of hearing: "One is like an Athenian and hearkeneth after news; if the preacher say anything of our armies beyond the sea, or Council at home, or matters at court. Another cometh to gaze about the church; he hath an evil eye which is still looking upon that from which Job did avert his eye. Another cometh to muse; so soon as he is set he falleth into a brown study; sometimes his mind runs on his market, sometimes on his journey, sometimes of his suit, sometimes of his dinner, sometimes of his sport after dinner, and the sermon is done before the man thinks where he is. Another cometh to hear, but so soon as the preacher hath said his prayer, he falls fast asleep, as though he had been brought in for a corpse, and the preacher should preach at his funeral." He is equally keen and sarcastic on those who admire the cleverness of a man who can take in his neighbors and make money at their expense: "He who can go beyond all in shifts and policy is counted the wisest man in court and city. Oh, if Machiavel had lived in our country what a monarch should he be! To what honor and wealth and power and credit might he have risen unto in short time, whether he had been a lawyer or a courtier, or a prelate! Methinks I see how many fingers would point at him in the streets and say, There goeth a deep fellow; he hath more wit in his little finger than the rest in their whole body."

From his character sketches here is one of the Flatterer: "He is like your shadow which doth imitate the action and gesture of your body, which stands when you stand, and walks when you walk, and sits when you sit, and riseth when you rise: so the flatterer doth praise when you praise, and finds fault when you find fault, and smiles when you smile, and frowns when you frown, and applauds you in your doings, and soothes you in your sayings, and in all things seeks to please your humor, till he hath sounded the depth of your devices, that he may betray you to your greatest enemies. As the sirens sing most sweetly when they intend your destruction, so flatterers speak most fair when they practise most treachery. Therefore every fair look is not to be liked, every smooth tale is not to be believed, and every glozing tongue is not to be trusted. We must try the words whether they come from the heart or no; and we must try the deeds whether they be answerable to the words or no."

On the more solemn aspects of life this

preacher can speak solemn and searching words, as for example, when he speaks of repentance as a matter of urgent need: "Whether thou be old or young, thy repentance cannot come too soon, because thy sin is gone before. If thou lackest a spur to make thee run, see how every day runneth away with thy life. Youth cometh upon childhood, age cometh upon youth, death cometh upon age, with such a swift sail, that if all our minutes were spent in mortifying ourselves, yet our glass would be run out before we had purged half our corruptions." These again are lurid and terrible words with which he describes the anguish of remorse: "There is a warning conscience and a gnawing conscience. The warning conscience cometh before sin, the gnawing conscience followeth after sin. The warning conscience is often lulled asleep, but the gnawing conscience wakeneth her again. If there be any hell in this world, they which feel the worm of conscience gnaw upon their hearts may truly say that they have felt the torments of hell. Who can express that man's horror but himself? Nay, what horrors are there which he cannot express himself? Sorrows are met in his soul at a feast; and fear, thought and anguish, divide his soul between them. All the furies of hell leap upon his heart like a stage. Thought calleth to fear; fear whistleth to horror; horror beckoneth to despair, and saith, Come and help me to torment the sinner. One saith that she cometh from this sin, and another saith that she cometh from that sin, so he goeth through a thousand deaths and cannot die."

Alongside of Henry Smith, and to be accounted even greater than he as a Puritan preacher, must be placed that Thomas Adams who has been called the Shakespeare of the Puritans. Southey seems to have been the one to start the comparison when he pronounced him to be the "prose Shakespeare of Puritan theologians, scarcely inferior to Fuller in wit or to Taylor in fancy." This judgment of Southey's may be qualified and at the same time extended by saying that while Adams is not so sustained as Jeremy Taylor nor so continuously sparkling as Thomas Fuller, he is surpassingly eloquent and much more thought-laden than either. He is like Shakespeare in one thing at least; while we have his works we know extremely little about the man himself. In 1612 he was a "preacher of God's Word at Willington," a village in Bedfordshire, four miles from Bedford town. And it may be noted by the way that a walk of twenty minutes from his vicarage door would have brought this Puritan Shakespeare to Cardington village, where, in the previous century, George Gascoigne, our earliest English satirist, was born, and that if he had extended his walk some fifteen minutes more he might have looked in at the cottage in Elstow parish where sixteen years later John Bunyan, our greatest English allegorist, first saw the light. Adams was afterwards vicar of Wingrave in Buckinghamshire and then preacher in one or two London churches, and when we have said this we have said nearly all that can be said to purpose about the man himself. It is with his work as "a preacher of God's Word," as he styles himself, rather than with his own personal history we are now concerned. As such we may describe him as one of the doctrinal Puritans, though he differed widely from many of the Puritans on the ecclesiastical and political questions of the time. Many of his sermons, like others of the period, were sermons on manners rather than on doctrine and lead us to think of him as a divine moralist rather than as a theologian. Yet a theologian he was, his theology being Calvinistic and Evangelical. He has a great belief that God will make that sure which we cannot make sure. He was not far wrong there, though we may not always be able to accept his way of stating this conviction of his as when he says that the Church is a number of men whom God hath set apart by an eternal decree. Still, he tempers even this when on the other side we find him saying: "It was not one for one that Christ died, not one for many: but one for all . . . and this one must needs be of infinite price." "Some affirm," says he, "that I have made the gate of heaven too narrow, and they hope to find it wider; God and the Scriptures are more merciful. True it is that heaven-gate is in itself wide enough and the narrowness is in respect of the man who enters; and though thy sins cannot make that too little to receive thee, yet they make thee too gross and unfit to get in."

As for the preacher himself, he would have him consecrate to the service all gifts and the ripest scholarship: "Learning," says he, "as well as office, is requisite for a minister. An unlearned scribe, without his treasure of old and new, is unfit to interpret God's oracles. The priest's lips shall preserve knowledge, is no less a precept to the minister than a promise to the people." Then, too, the life must correspond to the teaching: "He that preaches well in his pulpit but lives disorderly out of it, is like a young scribbler: what he writes fair with his hand, his sleeve comes after and blots." He who serves Christ must not be too eager after the applause of man: "I do not call thee aside to ask with what applause this sermon passeth, but (it is all I would have and hear) with what benefit? I had rather convert one soul than have a hundred praise me."

In a sermon on the Fatal Banquet to which Satan invites his guests, he has, he says, many bidders to his feast. Take a short muster of these inviters, these bidders to this banquet of vanity: they have all their several stands. In the Court he hath set *Ambition* to watch for base minds, that would stoop to any villany for preferment, and to bring them to this feast. This is a principal bidder. In the Law Courts he sets inviters that beckon contention to them, and fill the world with broils. I mean the libels of the law, pettifoggers, Satan's firebrands which he casteth abroad to make himself sport, and who do more hurt among the barley, the commons of this land, than Samson's foxes with the fire at their tails. "Oh," says he, "that they were shipped out for Virginia, for they cannot live without making broils" — which is a little hard upon Virginia, as we cannot but think. *Pride* is another bidder, and keeps a shop in the city. You shall find a description of her shop and take an inventory of her wares from the prophet — "the tinkling ornaments, the cauls, and the moon-tires." She sits upon the stall, and courts the passengers with a *What lack ye?* "Making a corner" in the market seems not to have been so modern an invention as we had supposed, for Adams tells us that *Engrossing* is another of Satan's inviters and hath a large walk; sometimes he watcheth the landing of a ship; sometimes he turns whole loads of corn besides the market. This bidder prevails with many a citizen, gentleman, farmer, and brings in infinite guests. *Bribery* too is an officious fellow, and a special bidder to this feast. He invites both forward and froward: the forward and yielding, by promises of good cheer, that they shall have a fair day of it; the backward honest man, by terrors and menaces that his cause shall else go westward. This kind of talk from Puritan books is now three centuries old, but I think you will feel with me there is a very modern ring about it and that it would not be much out of place even in some of the pulpits of to-day.

We remember how Shakespeare makes Hamlet exclaim, "What a piece of work is a man! how noble in reason! how infinite in faculty! in form and moving how express and admirable!" Here is an exclamation by this other Shakespeare — this Shakespeare among the Puritans, not unworthy to stand beside it. "Oh, how goodly this building of man appears when it is clothed with beauty and honor! A face full of majesty, the throne of comeliness wherein the whiteness of the lily contends with the sanguine of the rose; an active hand, an erected countenance, an eye sparkling out lustre, a smooth complexion arising from an excellent temperature and composition. Oh, what a workman was this, that could raise such a fabric out of the earth, and lay such orient colors upon dust!"

Yet on the other hand this same preacher has to pour forth his sorrowful lament that a being so nobly formed as man should yet spiritually be so insensible. "Isaiah," he says, "had not more cause for Israel than we for England to cry — 'We have labored in vain, and spent our strength for nought.' We give God the worst of all things that hath given us the best of all things. We give God measure for measure, but after an ill manner. For His blessings 'heapen and shaken and thrust together,' our iniquities 'pressed down and yet running over.'" With his pleading words we will close our words to-day: "Come, then, beloved to Jesus Christ, come freely, come betimes. The flesh calls, we come; vanity calls, we flock; the world calls, we fly; let Christ call early and late, He has yet to say: 'Ye will not come unto me that ye might have life.'"

IV

THOMAS GOODWIN AND THE CAMBRIDGE PLATONISTS

LECTURE IV

THOMAS GOODWIN AND THE CAMBRIDGE PLATONISTS

IN the last lecture our thoughts were turned to the sermons of two eminent preachers of Puritan times — Henry Smith, "the silver-tongued," and Thomas Adams, "the Shakespeare of the Puritans." While these sermons, however, are notable examples of intellectual and oratorical power, perhaps they can scarcely be accepted as typical illustrations of the ordinary Puritan discourse which was more doctrinal in form, and in spirit more experimental and evangelical. Coleridge said of certain Anglican authors that the cross shines but dimly in their writings, and this remark would apply to some extent to the two men just named. For more characteristic types of the Puritan of the first half of the seventeenth century we should do better to turn to such men as Robert Bolton, the author of "The Four Last Things," or to Richard Sibbes, the writer of the book entitled

"The Bruised Reed." But perhaps a better example than even these may be found in the person of Dr. Thomas Goodwin, whose discourses and treatises in many volumes have come down to us. During his life-time he filled various positions of influence. After being a student of Christ's College, Cambridge, and a Fellow of Catherine Hall, he became a licensed preacher of the University, a London pastor, a member of the Westminster Assembly of Divines, and, under the Protectorate of Cromwell, President of Magdalen College, Oxford. It was by the merest chance that at one time he did not take his place among the Puritan Fathers of New England. Receiving in 1647 an urgent invitation from John Cotton of Boston to come and labor with him, he so far yielded as to secure his passage; a large part of his valuable library was actually on board the vessel; and it was only at the last moment that the earnest entreaties of an attached people prevailed with him to remain among them as their pastor.

Naturally a preacher's own religious experience largely determines the style of his preaching. Thomas Goodwin had been brought to God in a way he could never forget. Comparing him with eminent contemporaries like John Owen and Richard Baxter, it has been said that Owen preached earnestly to the understanding, reasoning from his critical and devout knowledge of Scripture; Baxter preached forcibly to the conscience, reasoning from the fitness of things; while Goodwin appealed to the spiritual affections, reasoning from his own religious experience and interpreting Scripture by the insight of a renewed heart. He has told us himself how a more than ordinarily definite and decisive religious experience influenced his religious beliefs, and disposed him to accept the decided, though not exaggerated Calvinism for which he was distinguished. It seemed to him that he was laid hold of by an invisible hand which he felt to be the hand of God, and from which he could not free himself. Urged one day by a fellow-collegian to enter a church where a sermon was to be preached, he says, "I was loath to go in, for I loved not preaching, especially not that kind of it which good men used, and which I thought to be dull stuff." But as other scholars were going in he went too, and once in, though he would have been glad to be out again, shame made him stay. "I was never," he says, "so loath to hear a sermon in my life;" yet that sermon, so unwillingly listened to, as it went on laid hold of heart and conscience, and changed all his life for him. Both in the conviction of sin, the entrance into forgiveness and peace, and in the making of a full surrender and consecration of himself, he seemed to be in other hands than his own. "I thought myself to be as one struck down by a mighty power. I was strangely guided in the dark. I was acted all along by the Spirit of God being upon me, and my thoughts passively held fixed. An abundant discovery was made to me of my inward lusts and concupiscence. This new sort of illumination gave discovery of my heart in all my sinnings, searched the lower rooms of my heart, as it were, with candles, as the prophet's phrase is."

As with the work of conviction, so with that of deliverance. In this, too, he felt himself in the hands of God. The word of promise, softly whispered to his soul, filled and possessed all the faculties of his being. He was borne up by an assurance that God would pardon all his sins, though never so great for boldness, hardness of heart and heinousness of sinning, as He had pardoned Paul. Yet further: in the effort after full surrender of himself, and perfect consecration of heart and life it seemed to him that he had but to stand still and see the salvation of God: "I observed of this work of God on my soul that there was nothing of constraint or force in it, but I was carried on with the most ready and willing mind, and what I did was what I chose to do. With the greatest freedom I parted with my sins, formerly as dear to me as the apple of my eye, yea, as my life, and resolved never to return to them more. And what I did was from deliberate choice; I considered what I was doing, and reckoned with myself what it would cost me to make this great alteration. What the world thought of these things hindered me not at all. The weeds that entangled me in those waters, I swam and broke through with as much ease as Samson did with his withes; for I was made a vassal and a captive to another binding, such as Paul speaks of."

Possibly to some people this may sound like old-world talk, which has grown obsolete in these later days. Even different Christian men may look upon and explain it differently. Still there is more in it of living reality and firm grasp of spiritual fact than some may be prepared to admit. And one thing is certain:

no man will ever understand how Puritan preaching laid hold of men as it did; made such heroic, courageous, commanding souls as it did, till he has accurately gauged a profound religious experience like that which Thomas Goodwin has laid bare for us in himself.

And now, it may lead to wholesome searchings of heart in those who are devoting their lives to the ministry if we follow Thomas Goodwin a step further and see the effect of this great spiritual change upon the deepest motives of his life. No one can put this as he has put it himself. "Having been," he says, "devoted by my parents for the work of the ministry, I considered what it was did serve most to the glory of God in the work of the ministry, and *that* overturned all the projects and designs of my heart hitherto, which were the dearest of all to me; so dear, that I would certainly rather not have lived than have forsaken that interest. The University in those times was addicted in their preaching to a vainglorious eloquence, wherein the wits did strive to exceed one another; and that which I most of all affected, in my foolish fancy, was to have preached, for the matter thereof, in the way that Dr. Senhouse of St.

John's, afterwards made bishop, did exceed all men in. I instance him to explain the way and model that I set up, because his sermons, five or six of them, are in print, and because it is the eminentest farrago of all sorts of flowers of wit that are found in any of the fathers, poets, histories, similitudes, or whatever has the elegancy of wit in it; and in the joining and disposing of these together, wit was the eminent orderer in a promiscuous way. His way I took for my pattern, not that I hoped to attain to the same perfection, but I set him up in my thoughts to imitate as much as I was able. . . But my heart, upon this my turning to God and setting his glory as my resolved end of all my actions and ways, did soon discover to me the unprofitableness of such a design; and I came to this resolved principle, that I would preach wholly and altogether sound and wholesome words, without affectation of wit and vanity of eloquence. And in the end, this project of wit and vainglory was wholly sunk in my heart, and I left all, and have continued in that purpose and practice these three-score years; and I never was so much as tempted to put in any of my own withered flowers that I had gathered, and valued more than diamonds, nor have they offered themselves to my memory to the bringing them into a sermon to this day, but I have preached what I thought was truly edifying, either for conversion, or bringing them up to eternal life."

These heart-utterances from the pen of an old man in the evening of an honored life, one feels are almost too sacred for public speech. They are rather to be pondered by the minister of Christ when he is alone with God and upon his knees. It is good for us, even though it humble us, to bare our hearts before the Lord, and ask ourselves what it is we really preach for. Is it to make a livelihood, or to display real or supposed abilities, or to indulge such pleasurable feeling as the orator may enjoy in some excited mood, or to win some passing applause and gratify a miserable vanity? The question of motive is vital to the minister of Christ. Even in ordinary life, purity and sincerity of intention carry power with them and no counterfeit can take their place. The light enshrined in the centre of the character is sure to reveal itself and shed its radiance over everything the man does. And while this is true of every man, it is especially true of the minister of Christ. Surely it is a solemn thing to speak for God, to set forth the cross of Christ to men who have but a little span of life to live, and to do this in a spirit of empty vanity, for our own glory rather than for His who sent us. How such a ministry must shrivel before the searching gaze of Him whose eyes are as a flame of fire! Let every man take heed not only *what* but *how* he builds upon the foundation. "For each man's work shall be made manifest: for the day shall declare it because it is revealed in fire; and the fire itself shall prove each man's work of what sort it is. If any man's work shall be burned he shall suffer loss: but he himself shall be saved; yet so as through fire."

The profound sense he had of the living presence of God with him, guiding his steps and shaping his deepest religious experience, led Thomas Goodwin, as we might expect, to concern himself in his preaching with the divine facts of revelation rather than with the subtleties of human speculation. There is a characteristic sermon of his entitled, "The Heart of Christ in Heaven to sinners on earth," which is a good example of his method. The purpose of this sermon was to make intensely real to the men to whom he spoke the Christ who had gone beyond the region of sight into the heavens — to make them feel that He was as closely one with them in sympathy, and personal relations of helpfulness as though they could look into His face. This is not an easy thing to accomplish; an eminently intellectual man of our time has indeed declared it to be impossible. In Dr. Dale's life there is the following quotation from Dr. Jowett, late Master of Balliol College, Oxford: "Is it possible," he asks, "to feel a personal attachment to Christ such as is prescribed by Thomas à Kempis? I think that it is impossible, and contrary to human nature that we should be able to concentrate our thoughts on a person scarcely known to us, who lived 1800 years ago." On the other hand, in the same biography, we are told that Dr. Dale was once writing an Easter sermon and when half-way through, the thought of the risen Lord broke in upon him as it had never done before. "Christ is alive," I said to myself; "alive! and then I paused; — alive! and then I paused again; alive! Can that really be true? living as really as I myself am? I got up and walked about repeating 'Christ is living! Christ is living!' At first it seemed strange and hardly true, but at last it came upon me as a burst of sudden glory; yes, Christ is living. It was to me a new discovery, I thought that all along I had believed it; but not until that moment did I feel sure about it. I then said, "My people shall know it; I shall preach about it again and again until they believe it as I do now.'" Now that which Dr. Dale resolved to set about doing for his people in Birmingham in the nineteenth century was precisely that which Thomas Goodwin set about doing for his people in London two centuries and a half before. The problem of the modern Englishman was that of the ancient Puritan — how to make the Christ of Eternity a living and helpful personality to men who had not seen Him. Let me in a few sentences show you how Thomas Goodwin sought to solve this problem.

Proceeding from the known to the unknown he demonstrated what Christ *is* to his followers now, from what we know He *was* to His disciples once. The first part of this demonstration is taken from Christ's last farewell to His disciples. With great tenderness of feeling he shows that Our Lord's symbolic act of washing the disciples' feet was meant as a token that, having loved His own which were in the world, He loved them to the end; and further that he would carry on in the heavens the purifying process he had foreshadowed on the earth. The expression by deed of the overflowing love there was in His heart was followed by expressions of the same thing in words. He told them that it was for their good He was leaving them; that they should not be left orphans, for He would send the Comforter; that meantime He would be preparing a place for them in the many mansions of the Father's House, and He would come again and receive them to Himself. Because He lived they should live also. He then presently goes apart and alone to His Father and speaks over all again unto Him that which He had said unto them, saying behind their backs *of them* as much as He had said before their faces *to them.*

The second stage of Goodwin's demonstration takes us from the scene of sacred feeling in the upper chamber before the Crucifixion to what took place immediately after the Resurrection. Though these disciples in the hour of crisis had forsaken Him and fled, and Peter had even foully denied Him yet His first word after his reappearance concerning them was "Go, tell my *brethren,*" even as Joseph said to those who had so cruelly wronged him — "I am Joseph your brother." Thus He owns them as brethren still. This was the message sent on to them beforehand; and when He came Himself His salutation was "Peace be unto you;" and later in that interview He repeats the salutation. Then too when He was leaving He further assured their hearts, for He lifted up His hands and blessed them. It was while He blessed them He was parted from them, and thus His last act was one of benediction.

Then, again, no sooner had He left them than He proceeded to make good the promise He had made when with them. The Spirit came down at Pentecost and the Apostles were enabled to work signs and wonders as He said they should. The two Apostles Paul and John, afterwards saw Him personally, receiving revelations of His unchanging interest in and love for those who were His. And His very last words in the very last book of Revelation were words of welcome. Earth calls upon heaven, and heaven calls upon earth as the prophet speaks. The bride from earth says unto Christ: "Come to me;" and the Spirit in the saints' hearts below say "Come" unto

Him also; and Christ cries out as loud from Heaven "Come" in answer unto this desire in them. What an echoing and answering of hearts and of desires—heaven and earth ring again of it!

All this Goodwin sets forth as the *external* demonstration of Christ's feeling for men, from which he passes to speak of the *internal* demonstration. By this he means the known feeling of Father, Son, and Spirit for man's salvation; the relationships of closest and most sacred kind among men by which Christ shadows forth his union with His own. He is the subject of all relations, which no creature is; and He is the pattern and exemplar of these relations, for they are all but copies of His. And what He has already suffered for His own makes them more dear to Him. What zealous love there was in the heart of Paul towards the converts he made; and what passionate devotion in the heart of Moses towards the people of Israel whom he led, and shall Christ be less devoted, less loving than they? We need never fear that Christ's great advancement in heaven should any whit alter His disposition: for this His very advancement engageth Him the more. Although He be entered into the heavens it is to be a high-priest there, so that the highest preferment that heaven itself can bestow upon Him engageth Him unto grace and mercy.

I need not pursue this examination further, though Thomas Goodwin himself carries his argument and demonstration into other departments of thought. Enough has been said to show how by the force of divine facts the men of the past sought to produce divine results in their appeals to men. Perhaps, also, enough has been said to show that the facts of divine revelation, when marshalled and set in order before the minds of men, are likely to be more powerful than mere speculations of ours, however ingenious. No doubt, sermons like those of Thomas Goodwin's, as read now on the printed page, have an archaic and old-world appearance about them to us because they were spoken in the language of the time. That kind of speech was in the air of the seventeenth century; and in this matter no man can overstep the limits of his time. He would be simply useless if he could. The only language which will reach men is that to which they are accustomed; and possibly our speech of to-day may sound as primitive and archaic to the men of three centuries hence as that of the men of the seventeenth century sounds to us. What we have to see to is that it shall be as effective.

And now, partly by way of contrast, and partly also for other reasons, let me introduce you to a body of religious teachers, who, while living in the same century as Thomas Goodwin, belonged to a widely different school of thought. Any study of Puritan preaching in the seventeenth century would be incomplete without some reference to that small body of remarkable men known as the "Cambridge Platonists," or, the "Sect of Latitude Men," or the "Latitudinarians," as they were variously called; including Benjamin Whichcote, Ralph Cudworth, Nathanael Culverwell, John Smith, and Henry More. Though separating themselves from much that was distinctively Puritan, they yet started from Puritanism and were greatly influenced by it. With the exception of Henry More they were all of Emmanuel College, which was founded with an object as openly Puritan as it was safe to confess, and on to the time of the Restoration it was the chosen resort of the Puritan party and the training-place of Puritan divines. It was there that Bradshaw, the president of the Court which condemned

Charles I., was bred; it was there, too, that Cromwell placed his ablest son, Henry; from it came Sir Philip Meadows, one of Cromwell's Latin Secretaries; and also a long list of ejected rectors and Nonconformist preachers. It was there, also, that John Harvard was trained and many other of those divines who sought over here that freedom in preaching they could not have in their own land.

The year 1644 marks the rise of the new school of Cambridge Platonists. In that year the Long Parliament having overthrown the Laudian party proceeded to remodel Cambridge University in a Puritan direction. John Cotton's Cousin, Anthony Tuckney, who succeeded him as Vicar of Boston, was made Master of Emmanuel; Dr. Hill who was of Emmanuel, and who also had been John Cotton's colleague at Boston, was placed at the head of Trinity College; and Benjamin Whichcote, who, in his undergraduate days, had had Anthony Tuckney as his tutor at Emmanuel, was made Provost of King's, succeeding Dr. Collins, who had been ejected by Parliament. Thus these friends, "very dear to each other," and all of them Emmanuel men, became the leading spirits, and largely the formative influence, of the University. Up to this point, therefore, we may assume that Benjamin Whichcote, afterwards the foremost man among the Cambridge Platonists, stood high in repute with the Puritan authorities of the time.

He is described as the great University preacher of the Commonwealth. What Chaderton and Perkins had been in the days of Elizabeth, Whichcote was half a century later. Archbishop Tillotson, in his younger days one of Whichcote's admirers, tells us that his regular Sunday afternoon lecture in the chapel of Trinity College drew crowds "not only of the young scholars, but of those of greater standing, and best repute for learning in the University," and that he contributed "more to the forming of the students of that University in a sober sense of religion than any man in that age." His great sphere of influence was the pulpit. He had the true oratorical temperament which is at its best when face to face with an audience. In preaching he used "no other than very short notes, not very legible," and, as with Frederick Robertson, the sermons we have of his were either printed from his own rough notes, or from shorthand reports of admiring hearers, and did not appear till after his death, the most complete edition being that published in Aberdeen as late as 1751.

So completely was Whichcote identified with the Puritans in public estimation that at the Restoration he shared the fate of the Puritan leaders, being removed from the provostship by especial order of the King. Yet on the other hand so widely had he separated from the Puritans in his theological system that in 1651 Anthony Tuckney who, as we have said, had been his tutor at Emmanuel, and who was his senior by ten years, felt it right seriously to remonstrate with him. In the autumn of that year Tuckney, writing to him, says: "I desire to be so ingenuous with you as out of that ancient and still continued love I bear you, to have leave to tell you that my heart hath been much exercised about you; and that especially since your being Vice-Chancellor I have seldom heard you preach but something hath been delivered by you, and that so authoritatively, and with the big words — sometimes of 'divinest reason,' and sometimes of 'more than mathematical demonstration' — that hath very much grieved me, and I believe others with me; and yesterday as much as any time."

As we read these words of the elder to the younger man, breathing an ancient affection and at the same time an anxious fear, we feel inclined to ask what are the matters in controversy between them? While both are regarded as Puritans by the authorities of the time, how is it that the Master of Emmanuel feels it his duty gravely to protest against the religious teaching of the Provost of King's, who is also Vice-Chancellor of the University? Is this one of those controversies which are now dead and done with, or is it one which has still important lessons for the preachers of our own time? For an answer to these questions let us briefly examine this Cambridge movement of the seventeenth century, and find out, if we can, what were its strong and attractive points, and in what directions its weakness lay.

That there were many attractive features about the Cambridge Platonists no one can deny who has at all caught the spirit of their lives and teaching. There is an undoubted charm about them while, as spectators of the world only through the loopholes of retreat, they dwelt upon the visions of the "supreme

Beautiful and Good," and left us a legacy of noble thoughts. We cannot but admire the calm philosophic spirit of men who "studied to propagate better thoughts, to take men off from being in parties, or from narrow notions, from superstitious conceits and a fierceness about opinions." In days when so many writers are pessimistic we cannot but envy the optimism of men who were wholly strangers to the gloom and the pain and the self-annihilation of other mystics; who permitted no clouds, no threatening darkness to dim their eyes as they ascend the hill of vision; and for whom, as it has been said, the prospect expands as they go on their way rejoicing, until the enlightened spirit sees the shady city of palm-trees, and beyond, the sparkling towers of the New Jerusalem.

The object of Whichcote and his followers was to unite philosophy and religion in their scheme of thought and to confirm the union on the indestructible basis of reason and the essential elements of our higher humanity. Their admirers claim for them that theirs was the first elaborate attempt to wed Christianity and philosophy made by any Protestant school, and indeed the first true attempt of the kind since the days of the great Alexandrine teachers. Their experiment therefore should be of the deepest interest to us who are preachers, who are convinced ourselves and wish to convince others, that the highest truths in revelation are conformable to the highest reason in man; that, as they put it, "nothing is true in divinity which is false in philosophy." Did they succeed, and if not, how may we account for their failure? As to the fact, at all events of his comparative failure, we have the admission of Whichcote's own admirers. It is admitted that he failed to influence English speculation permanently; that, while he inspired his hearers, men of great and varied power — Smith and More, Worthington and Cudworth, Patrick and Tillotson, he founded no school, and left no successors in the third generation. My own impression is that if his influence lingered on into the eighteenth century it merely strengthened that cold rationalism which for nearly a whole century went far towards killing all spiritual religion in the Church of England. The causes of failure are not without instruction to the preachers of to-day. Let me briefly point out what they were.

1. It appears to me that Whichcote did

not sufficiently discriminate between man's natural reason and his spiritual faculty. We should all be disposed to accept his central principle, which was — the essential unity of all truth, natural and revealed, and its affinity to the constitution of man. We should maintain with him that whatsoever things are to be found in any of the wise teachers of the past, that are true, were in God before they were in them, and have their place in that Kingdom of truth, of which our Lord is King. We quite go with him too when he says that "a man has as much right to use his own understanding in judging of truth, as he has a right to use his own eyes to see his way;" and we feel that he utters a pungent truth which all preachers would do well to remember when he says: "I have always found that such preaching of others hath most commanded my heart which hath most illuminated my head." But we pause and dissent when in the matter of the religious life he so glorifies the natural reason as to say that "to go against reason is to go against God;" that it "is the Divine Governor of man's life; it is the very voice of God;" that it "discovers what is natural, and receives what is supernatural." On *philosophical* grounds we should be disposed to argue with Martineau that we cannot credit the intellect with the moral apprehensions; that there is nothing in the mere presence of intelligence to supply the defect of moral consciousness; and that the moral sentiments cannot be resolved into modes of intellectual apprehension and deduced from the essentials of Reason. For knowledge is the apprehension of *what is*, while morality (on its cognitive side) is the apprehension of what *ought to be*—and these are different spheres. Then, too, on *religious* grounds Whichcote's theory will not stand the test of facts. He meant by 'reason' very much what Paul meant by 'wisdom' and Paul affirms that after centuries of experiment it was clearly proved that "the world through its wisdom knew not God." After all, experience goes to show that "spiritual things are spiritually discerned," and the sin of man's life has an awful power in dimming, and even in destroying, his spiritual discernment. Since men while knowing God, glorified Him not as God, they became vain in their reasonings and their senseless heart was darkened. Before man's reason, therefore, can become a perfect instrument for the discovery of spiritual truth man himself must be spiritually reconstructed and divinely illuminated.

2. Another explanation of Whichcote's comparative failure is to be found in the fact that he sacrificed, or at least minimized, important truths in order to secure intellectual unity of expression. His system of thought was a reaction from that of Puritanism, which had become too rigid and creed-bound, and the tendency of all reaction is to go to an opposite extreme. In the second stage of the Reformation the principle of authority in the Church had too much superseded the principle of enquiry; and Whichcote felt that Theology as systematized with logical precision in the Westminster Confession was not the final word. It did not entirely cover, or completely meet, the actual facts of daily experience. It seemed to him, therefore, that the real test ot truth of which he was in search was to be found in character and conduct, that truth was the soul in action. For the formula: "I think, therefore I am" he would substitute: "I act, therefore I am;" "I do, therefore I have being," and affirmed that it is by action answering to knowledge that character is slowly shaped according to

an inevitable law. This being so, he would have said, Let us not trouble ourselves about dogma, let us unite in worship. Unity of religious opinion is evidently impossible; there is the more need, therefore, of community of religious life. The true Church is not the Church resting in this creed or that, proclaiming this type of doctrine or that, but the company of the faithful owning Christ as their Lord. The Church subsists in communion of spirit, not in coincidence of doctrine. It has a common faith — it may have a common worship; but it is not bound to any definite type of theology — any argumentative or theoretic creed.

Coleridge said that the Cambridge Platonists were not so much Platonists as Plotinists and here is one of the signs of it. For Neo-Platonism sought to reduce all forms of truth to one general amalgam. Plotinus, looking round upon Platonist and Aristotelian, Sophist and Sensualist, Epicurean and Stoic, would have said: "Repudiate these partial scholars. Leave them to their disputes, pass over their systems, already tottering for lack of a foundation, and be it yours to show how their teachers join hands above them. In such a spirit of reverent enthusiasm you may attain a higher unity. You mount in speculation, and from that height ordain all nobler actions for your lower life." Again the same thing was repeated when in the fifteenth century there was in Florence a revival of Neo-Platonism under Gemisthus Pletho and his companions, Nicholas of Cusa and Pico of Mirandola. These men dreamed that it was possible to set up a philosophic worship, emasculated and universal which should harmonize in a common vagueness all the religions of the world. It has been well said that they forgot that lip-homage paid to all religions is a virtual denial of each, and that it is possible so to combine religion and philosophy as to rob philosophy of its only principle and religion of its only power. It was so in another form with the Cambridge Platonists. The attempt to separate religious worship from religious conviction landed them in intellectual unreality. Contemporary writers dwell upon the hearty subscription which these men gave to the Thirty-nine Articles of the Church of England. But it turns out that this hearty subscription was very much like that which John Henry Newman gave to these same Articles some two centuries later when in Tract No. XC. he showed that they meant only what he personally wanted them to mean. The subscription of these Cambridge divines merely implied acceptance of the Articles as "instruments of peace." Bishop Fowler defends this unreality — we may go further and say this double-dealing — by quoting these ominous words from Archbishop Ussher: "We do not suffer any man to reject the Thirty-nine Articles of the Church of England at his pleasure; yet neither do we look upon them as essentials of saving faith, or legacies of Christ and His Apostles; but in a mean, as pious opinions fitted for the preservation of unity: neither do we oblige any man to *believe* them, but only not to *contradict* them." You will probably feel with me that this kind of talk is not calculated to win our respect, and that if a man in ordinary business signed a contract in the easy-going fashion in which these men are said to have subscribed the Articles we should know what to think of him.

All this has its instructive side for the preachers of to-day. It shows us that nothing permanently succeeds in the way of religious teaching except a clear and unreserved setting forth of the distinctive facts and truths of God's own revelation. Every true man, of course, will try to see these facts and truths with his own eyes but he must never substitute his own speculations, however original and ingenious, for the authoritative revelations of God. To the extent to which he yields to this temptation his ministry will be powerless. Man's speculations change with changing times, but the Word of the Lord endureth forever. Thrice has the effort been made to render the abstractions of a philosophized religion a power among men, and thrice it has failed. Earnest-minded men feel that it is puerile and powerless, and they will have none of it; while the careless and superstitious remain careless and superstitious still. Man's passions and worldliness of heart are not to be beaten down by mere straws of our making. They can only be overcome by that which has God's own power in it. For a preacher to refine away what is most distinctive of divine revelation and then to subtilize the rest into a mere sentimental theism is to court predestined failure. It has been tried under the most favorable conditions by some of the ablest and most learned of men. If it failed in their hands, and it did fail, it is not likely to succeed with others. A religion that can only live in the study and on the heights of intellectual speculation, that demands philosophic culture as an indispensable condition may suit men of an aristocratic spirit, but it will never meet the wants of the great body of the people who, often under hard and sorrowful conditions, are fighting the battle of life. There is room and need in the Christian pulpit for the loftiest genius and the profoundest learning, but the word to be delivered must be that which went forth from the carpenter's lowly roof, and was first published abroad by fishermen and tent-makers of old.

V

JOHN BUNYAN AS A LIFE-STUDY FOR PREACHERS

LECTURE V

JOHN BUNYAN AS A LIFE-STUDY FOR PREACHERS

HITHERTO in these lectures we have followed the unfoldings of Puritanism, so far as the preaching of the Puritans was concerned, on to the middle of the seventeenth century. To-day we pass from the Commonwealth period to that which followed the Restoration of the monarchy in England, during which, through the passing of the Act of Uniformity in 1662, Puritanism almost ceased to be described as such and came to be more generally known as Nonconformity. Looked at on one side — the side of the sufferings and hardships endured, the twenty-eight years between 1660, the year of the Restoration, and 1688, the year of the Great Revolution, may be described as the period of the wilderness wandering of the Church of God in England. Looked at on the other side — the side which displayed the bravery and steadfastness of the men who were loyal to conscience, even to bonds and imprisonment, it may be described as the heroic period of Free Church life. The men who mainly were the makers of that period are eminently worthy of our consideration also from the point of view of the preacher and the pastor: I propose, therefore, setting some of the foremost of them before you for purposes of suggestion and instruction. As to who shall be the first of these, the choice seems largely determined for me by my own personal surroundings. For the last five-and-thirty years I have had the honor to be the minister of the church at Bedford of which John Bunyan was minister during the last sixteen years of his life. As circumstances have thus made me somewhat familiar with the work he did and the spirit in which he did it, I ventured to think that you would not be impatient with me if before you who are to be ministers of Christ, I were to set forth *John Bunyan as a life-study for preachers.*

The methods of great artists are charged with instruction for those to whom Art is to be the masterwork of life. It is the province of genius to touch life livingly, as by a sort of instinct, to open out new paths of light which other feet may traverse. No doubt every man will do his best work by simply being himself, and no mere copy of some one else. Imitations are usually failures. Still, even the most original artist may find it worth while to make a study of color and form as exemplified in the best works of the Great Masters; and true men may receive stimulus and help by carefully noting how true men have done their work before them. John Bunyan is chiefly thought of as a Dreamer of wonderful dreams, but he was also, as his contemporaries have told us, one of the most living preachers England has ever known. His own intense religious experience largely aided his genius in this. As he tells us himself, he had tarried long at Sinai to see the fire and the cloud and the darkness, that he might fear the Lord all the days of his life upon earth, and tell of his wonders to others. So that when, in after days, he spoke with kindling eye and tongue of fire the things he had seen and felt, men bent to his words as the corn bends to the wind. No piler-up of mere rhetoric was this Dreamer of Bedford, but one deeply learned in the lore of human souls, heaven-taught in the great and wonderful art of laying hold of men.

It so happens that in the memorable

Dream by which Bunyan will always be best known he has in several ways given us his conception of what the minister of Christ ought to be and to do. Few things are more characteristic of this man than the high ideal he had formed for himself of the office and work of the Christian minister. It was not the ecclesiastical greatness of the man which impressed him, for he had a withering scorn for the mere priest, for those unreal men who had come into the priest's office for a piece of bread and whom he was wont to describe as 'the carnal ministry' — not the ecclesiastical greatness of the man as a mere official, but the greatness of his work as one dealing with human souls as the messenger of God. Of this work, I say, Bunyan had a very high ideal, let me first show you what that ideal was, as we gather it from various scenes and characters in his Pilgrim story, and then let us see how he worked out his ideal in his own life and ministry.

You will remember that part of the Pilgrim's Progress where Christian arrives at the house of the Interpreter. "Come in," said the Interpreter, "I will show thee what will be profitable to thee." Whereupon he had him into a private room and bid his man open a door — "the which when he had done, Christian saw the picture of a very grave person hang up against the wall; and this was the fashion of it: It had eyes uplift to Heaven, the best of Books in his hand, the law of Truth was written upon his lips, the world was behind his back; it stood as if it pleaded with men, and a crown of gold did hang over its head." When, five-and-twenty years ago, a statue of Bunyan was set up to his honor in Bedford town, the sculptor took that picture from the House of the Interpreter and embodied it in the bronze statue. So to all passers-by to-day Bunyan in his effigy stands there with eyes uplift to Heaven, the best of Books in his hand, and as if he pleaded with men. Thus, so far as sculpture is concerned, he is made to realize his own ideal, which, also in life, he largely did. "What means this?" asks Christian, as he looks at that picture on the wall. Let us, in a sentence or two, see what it means:

The Preacher, as Bunyan conceives of him, "has eyes lifted up to Heaven," for from thence comes his commission, and from thence also his sufficiency and strength: "The best of Books is in hand," for he is the setter-forth of a divine revelation: "his work is to know and unfold dark things to sinners;" he has not to tell men merely what he thinks, but what God thinks, what God has said and done. "The law of truth is written upon his lips," for he aims ever at reality, he is a genuine man through and through, transparently sincere, having no faith in pious make-believes, or unreality of any sort or kind. "The world is behind his back;" which is as much as to say that the spirit of the world is not his spirit, its ambitions are not his, and the rewards it can offer have little attraction for him, for a greater world is risen to his view, and the less fades before the greater. "He stands as if he pleaded with men;" he has in his heart the love, the divine compassion for men which were in Christ's heart; he pleads with them for their own souls' sake, and for the sake of Him who died for their souls—pleads as the mother pleads with her boy whom she loves as her own life. Finally, over the head of the man seen in the Picture "there did hang a crown of gold; that is to show thee that, slighting and despising the things that are present, for the love that he hath to his Master's service, he is sure in the world that comes next to have glory for his reward."

When the long day's work is done and "the Chief Shepherd shall appear ye shall receive the crown of glory that fadeth not away." May I not, as I pass on, say to every Divinity student what the Interpreter said to Christian —"Wherefore take good heed to what I have showed thee, and bear well in thy mind what thou hast seen."

But besides this instructive picture on the wall, in the Pilgrim's Progress Bunyan presents a many-sided ministry in action and life. He supplements that picture by a varied succession of characters which appear on the scene of his story, and sustain helpful relations to one and another of the many pilgrims whom we see on their way to the City of God. First we have *Evangelist*, who is the Christian Minister scarcely, if at all, transformed by the requirements of the allegory. As his name implies, he is the proclaimer of an Evangel, he has good tidings to tell. The story opens before us with the sight of a man greatly distressed in mind, and out of whose lips as he wanders the fields there comes the pitiful cry, "What must I do to be saved?" He is, he says, not willing to die nor able to come to judgment, and he is afraid the burden upon his back will sink him lower than the grave. This is the sort of man with whom, of all others, Evangelist loves to deal. With brotherly heart he says to him — "Do you see yonder wicket gate? No. Then do you see yonder shining light? You think you do. Well, keep that light in your eye and follow it till you see the gate." There you have the Christian Minister in the character in which I trust it will be the pleasure of your own life to be found through the years God may spare you to work for Him — as the guide of sin-stricken, salvation-seeking souls. All things are of God, who reconciled us to Himself through Christ, and gave unto us the ministry of reconciliation.

And now let me take you to the Palace Beautiful for another phase of your life-work as the ministers of Christ. There at the gate stands *Watchful*, the porter, with kindly word giving welcome to the man who, with timid, trembling step, has just come past the lions in the way. Before introducing the pilgrim to the rest of the household he has free and friendly talk with him; finds out what sort of man he is, where he comes from, and whither he is bound. So that in *Watchful* we have the Christian minister in his function as president of the church; feeling himself responsible, as to some extent he is responsible, for the spiritual character of the community committed to his charge. He is right brotherly and kind, still his name is Watchful. He knows that he is only a steward, and that it is required in stewards that a man be found faithful. He is conscious that he has no authority to make a church of Christ other than Christ meant it to be: and he is aware that when churches cease to be made up of spiritual men they cease to be churches at all; that if you bring the world into the Church you have destroyed the Church and you have not benefited the world; that if the salt have lost its savor there is nothing on earth more pungent than itself to give it back its saltness.

Yet again: while the minister of Christ is to be *Evangelist*, the proclaimer of truth, and *Watchful*, the porter at the gate, he is also to sustain certain important relations towards the brotherhood within. He must be a man among men, the guide of pilgrims, the champion of right, the consoler of sorrow, the inspirer of hope — in short, according to Bunyan's idea, he must be the *Greatheart* of the Christian pilgrimage. Mr. Greatheart is the man-servant of Interpreter, the guide, conductor, and protector of pilgrims: "I am," said he, "at my Lord's commandment. I have it in commission to comfort the feeble-minded, to support the weak." Other work also has he to do at times, not more manly, but more resolute, for again and again there comes to him the call to go into action against wrong. "I have a commandment to resist sin, to overcome evil, to fight the good fight of faith." The Christian pastor, then, in the character of Greatheart, is to be the leader of men, as manly as he is Christian, humanly touching life at all points, a living, large-hearted man among living men, women, and children. While being the preacher and teacher he is also to be the spiritual guide of human souls amidst the perils and perplexities of their pilgrimage. It is a great gift, and a greater privilege to be this wisely, and men are grateful indeed when they meet a real man, who, to use George Foxe's phrase, can speak to their condition. Some men who are not ministers have this gift, and there are ministers who have it not. There is a divine art in dealing with men not to be learnt all at once, not to be acquired in lecture halls or from books, but on your knees in communion with God, and in the daily experiences of life in living sympathy with men. It comes only in its fulness with the process of years, and with deepening heart-experiences of our own. It requires a large and varied knowledge of men, their motives, their sorrows, their temptations. The man who can do this well must be both loving and wise — loving with the love of Christ, wise with the wisdom of God.

There is also another side to Greatheart's work: while he is to be the spiritual *guide*, he is also to be the spiritual *warrior*, fighting with weapons of proof the battles of the Lord. The Episcopal Church, established by law in England, makes it its boast that, sending forth its clergy, it places "a *gentleman* in every parish." That may be a good thing or it may not. Everything depends upon who and what-like the gentleman is. On the whole it may be safer for our churches to try to place in every community a *true man*, who, as opportunity offers, shall show himself on the side of the oppressed, and speak up for every righteous cause. Every here and there on the road to the Celestial City there are powerful enemies lying in wait; it is well, therefore, that there should be on the road also a man with manhood enough in him to challenge them, to confront them with some hope of victory, to proclaim the divine authority of right over wrong.

If you have followed me thus far; have taken into your mental vision that picture hanging upon the wall in the Interpreter's House; and have placed alongside it the characters of Evangelist, Watchful and Great-heart, you will have nearly realized to yourselves Bunyan's conception of the ideal Christian minister,—nearly but not quite. One other scene from the Pilgrim story is still needed to complete the whole. When Christian and Hopeful arrived at the Delectable Mountains, where were gardens and orchards, vineyards and fountains of water, they found there Shepherds feeding their flocks. The Pilgrims, going to them "and leaning upon their staves (as is common with weary Pilgrims, when they stand to talk with any by the way)," asked what mountains these were and whose were the sheep that fed upon them. In reply the Shepherds told them that these mountains are Emmanuel's Land, within sight of the City, that the sheep feeding on them are His, and that He laid down his life for them. Further, the Shepherds said that the Lord of these mountains had given them a charge, not to be forgetful to entertain strangers: therefore the good of the place was before them. The names of these Shepherds were *Knowledge*, *Experience*, *Watchful*, and *Sincere*. This is a pastoral scene, quiet and restful, the meaning of which it is not easy to miss. These Shepherds are pastors of the flock of Christ, and their four names denote four qualities, all of which should be found in every good minister of Jesus Christ. And, whereas the other names we have had before us — Evangelist, Watchful, Greatheart, set forth the outward activities of the minister's life, these names, Knowledge, Experience, Watchful, and Sincere, describe the inward qualities and spiritual equipments of the man divinely called to feed the flock of God.

He is to have *Knowledge*, the learning, the intelligence obviously required to feed the people of God with knowledge and understanding. He is to have a mind ever alert to see and learn, especially the best things, intermeddling with all wisdom, especially that which relates to God and things of God. Then, too, he must acquire *Experience*. It is dear-bought. It can only come through undergoing temptation, trial, heart-sorrow. But it is worth all it costs, for it brightens many a Scripture otherwise obscure, sends a thrill through many a prayer, and wings many an arrow to the conscience. He is also to be *Watchful*. He who bore that name as porter of the Palace Beautiful was to watch over the Church and its arrangements without; this man of the same name is to keep guard over heart and life within. He is to watch over his own soul, and also to watch for the souls of his people — to watch as they that must give account. Finally he must be *Sincere*. Simplicity and purity of intention in him will soon be felt by his people and will give him wonderful power over their hearts. They will let him say anything to them when once they are sure that he is real and that he loves them. "In holiness and sincerity of God," says the Apostle, "we behaved ourselves in the world, and more abundantly to you-ward" — no unreal words on the lips in daily converse; no false fire on the altar in prayer and sermon, no affectation of a sympathy the heart does not feel!

And now, having thus given you, from Bunyan's Dream, Bunyan's ideal of the minister of Christ, let us turn to see how he tried to realize that ideal in his own life and ministry.

First, let us see how he tried to realize it in his *preaching*. As to literary form Bunyan's sermons naturally took much of their character from the time in which he lived. But while these were arranged after a seventeenth-century manner there was that about them which was peculiarly his own. To begin with, he was a master of grand and noble Saxon speech. It came to him as naturally as song to a bird. And it was not meant for mere rhetorical display. He meant to do something with his sermons when he had made them. He was bent on seeing spiritual realities for himself and on making other people see them. He would take nothing at second-hand. Lithographed ser mons, such as so many of the English clergy buy at so much a dozen, would not have been in his way. Says he: "I never endeavored to, nor durst make use of other men's lines (though I condemn not all that do), for I verily thought and found by experience that what was taught me by the Word and Spirit of Christ could be spoken, maintained and stood to by the soundest and best established conscience." He sought, as we all should, to stand on reality in everything. To Him both sin and salvation were as real as the very earth on which He trod. As He spoke of sin He spoke of it with a shudder such as that with which men speak of a danger from which they have barely escaped with their lives. This part of my work," he says, "I fulfilled with great sense; for the terrors of the Law and guilt for my transgression lay heavy on my conscience. I preached what I felt, what I smartingly did feel, even that under which my poor soul did groan and tremble to astonishment. Indeed I have been as one sent unto them from the dead. I went myself in chains to preach to them in chains; and carried that Fire in my own conscience that I persuaded them to beware of." So also, when he passed from conflict to the calm of soul which forgiveness brings, he was just as real. "When the Lord came upon my soul with some staid peace and comfort through Christ, then too I still preached what I saw and felt." In this intense directness and reality lay the secret of this man's power. He found his way to other men's hearts because he spoke so truly out of his own. He not only told the truth, but he made the truth to tell. Said a preacher who knew how to do it himself, there must be that in our sermons which will both strike and stick. A man may *part* with truth and not *communicate* it. An important part of communication is reception, and that may not have taken place. An arrow all wing but no point is worthless. Augustine was determined to get right into the minds of the people to whom he spoke. "I would rather," said he, "that the grammarians should criticise me than that my people should not understand me." An important rule to bear in mind is that you must keep touch with your audience and carry them along with you. Said Alexander VIII. to Cardinal Polignac, "You always commence by agreeing with me, and you finish by making me agree with you." There is nothing so unreal as to see a man speaking *before* his hearers but not *to* them. Some men get into an unreal professional way of speaking in public. In private converse they are very sensible men and worth listening to, but directly they get on to their feet their common sense seems to have left them. Said a Frenchman of his priest, "When M. le Curé gives advice he does it admirably, but when he wishes to make a sermon he is unbearable." "Now doctor," said a shrewd-witted patient, "don't be professional but tell me the truth." Archbishop Magee used to say that all preachers may be divided into three classes — preachers you cannot listen to, preachers you can listen to and preachers you cannot help listening to. Judging from his writings and from what his contemporaries have told us of him, Bunyan belonged to that class of preachers men cannot help listening to. His reading and thinking, his experience of life and knowledge of men, his observation of character in the forming and of motive in the working — all were made to bear on the great work on which his heart was set and to which his life was consecrated. A ministry having such elements of power and reality will be successful in this century as well as in the seventeenth; while mere made-up men, pieces of artificiality and officialism, preachers who say things merely because they are expected to say them, will be successful in none of the centuries and if the truth must be told they do not deserve to be.

Simplicity and directness of speech are great qualities in a preacher. It does not require much genius, so to speak, as that no man can for the life of him make out what you are driving at. It is a mark of real power when you can so put a thing as that one man shall wonder that he never saw the subject in that light before, and to another it shall seem so simple and obvious that he falls into the natural mistake of supposing that he could have preached that sermon himself. It is a difficult problem, no doubt, and one that every preacher has had to face, how to speak to a miscellaneous audience so as to secure the interest of widely different orders of mind. There can be no better aim for a preacher than to try so to present the truth of God that the common people shall hear him gladly, and at the same time the most intelligent members of his congregation shall feel that their understandings have been respected and their interest secured. "*Think* with the wise," said Aristotle, "but *speak* with the common people."

On the matter of literary form we may note that Bunyan seems carefully to have avoided one sin not easily forgiven — the cardinal sin of dulness. Neither in his character sketches nor in his illustrations does he ever grow tedious. The various people in his allegories step out into the open — they interest you or they amuse you, or they instruct you; there is one thing they never do, they never weary you. They do all they were meant to do and then they disappear. Yet in that brief space they have left a distinct impression of their own individuality upon you. Many of the illustrations in his sermons, too, are simply exquisite. Take for example this of Christian fellowship: "Christians are like the several flowers in a garden that have upon each of them the dew of heaven, which being shaken with the wind, they let fall their dew at each other's roots, whereby they are jointly nourished and become nourishers of each other." That is an illustration which is a word-picture, a poem in prose. The most refined feel the charm of it, and the plainest man is conscious of its beauty and force. Moreover it is an illustration which is not dragged in for its own sake. It really does illustrate, that is, it throws light on the subject in hand. Moreover it is not overdone. It leaves off at the precise point at which it ought to stop. It is well sometimes to have the moral courage to leave out something. The leaving out may really increase the value of that which remains in. There are times when the half turns out to be more than the whole.

Then, again, in realizing his own ideal as a

preacher, Bunyan tells us that he intentionally laid the chief stress on universal and central truths. One of the first things that strikes us about the Pilgrim's Progress is its universality. Dean Stanley said of it that "it is one of the few books which act as a religious bond to the whole of Christendom; that it is, perhaps with six others, and equally with any of those six, the book which, after the English Bible, has contributed to the common religious culture of the Anglo-Saxon race." The forms which rise before us are essentially representative in their character. While drawn from the ordinary middle-class burghers of an ordinary Midland town in the seventeenth century, men of all nationalities consent to recognize them as fellow-citizens and contemporaries. Not only were they living in Bunyan's time, they are living still. Only a little time ago I travelled myself with that brisk young man Ignorance from the country of Conceit. Pliable is to be found in many a congregation. Talkative does not confine himself to any one of the Christian denominations. Mr. Facing-both-ways found his way into the British Parliament at the very last election; and for anything I know he may also be met with in Senate and Congress, even in the United

States. Mr. By-ends has not ceased to be a prominent figure in certain religious circles. He is still true to his old principle, which is never to go against wind and tide; he still likes Religion best when she goes in the sunshine and walks in silver slippers; and his grandfather the waterman still gets his living by looking one way and rowing another. And if such men as these are with us still, so also are others of widely different sort. Christian, still faring forward, through storm and sunshine, to the city of God; Faithful still staunch and true even in Vanity Fair; Hopeful with his word of sympathy and cheer even in the dungeons of Doubting Castle; Standfast, still winning victories upon his knees; Mr. Fearing, timid, trembling soul, not afraid of the lions, but only afraid of his acceptance at last; Old Honest, too, sturdy as an oak, and true as steel — we know them all, for they are all with us, and all represent types of character which are permanent and world-wide.

And as with the characters Bunyan depicted so with the truths he most of all delighted to preach — they were permanent and universal also. He aimed mainly, he tells us, at that which was central and vital. "I did labor with great diligence and earnestness," he says, "to find out such a word as might, if God would bless, lay hold of and awaken the conscience." Elsewhere also he says: "I never cared to meddle with things that were controverted, and in dispute among the saints, especially things of the lowest nature; yet it pleased me much to contend with great earnestness for the Word of Faith and the remission of sins by the Death and Sufferings of Jesus; but I say as to other things I should let them alone, because I saw they engendered strife, and because that they, neither in doing nor in leaving undone, did commend us to God to be His." Take this again: "It pleased me nothing to see people drink in opinions if they seemed ignorant of Jesus Christ, and the worth of their own salvation, sound conviction for sin, especially for unbelief, and a heart set on fire to be saved by Christ, with strong breathings after a truly sanctified soul. That it was that delighted me; those were the souls I counted blessed." There is much of wisdom in all this, in keeping truth in true perspective, and in giving their due prominence to the mountain heights of Scripture and of human life.

Further, while Bunyan aimed at central things in his teaching, he spoke of them with an honest ring of clear conviction. No preacher of doubts was he, but of divine certainties. In his view a man who has no convictions of his own, no living grasp of God's truth, was an impertinence in the pulpit and something worse. "I have been in my preaching," says he, "especially when engaged in the doctrine of life by Christ, as if an angel of God had stood at my back to encourage me. Oh, it hath been with such power and heavenly evidence upon my own soul, while I have been laboring to unfold it, to demonstrate it, and to fasten it upon the conscience of others, that I could not be contented with saying *I believe and am sure;* methought I was *more than sure* (if it be lawful so to express myself) that those things which I then asserted were true." Now herein lay part of the secret of this man's power as a preacher. Let me not be misunderstood. There is a vain-confidence of ignorance as well as an assured conviction of faith, and we must not mistake the one for the other. But there is another side to the question. There is great outcry now and again against dogmatism by some very dogmatic people, and there are cases, no doubt, where a man may be too sure, but on great questions, and in the ministry of the Gospel some men fail beeause they are not sure enough. There are, of course, some moot questions on which an honest man may think it best to keep an open mind; such questions, for example, as those which relate to the literary structure, date or authorship of certain books of Scripture. All that we want to get at in these matters is the truth, whether it squares with our preconceived opinions or not. For in the long run the truth will always turn out to be our best friend and truest helper. But on central verities — on God and Christ and the Divine Spirit, on sin and salvation, on the formation of character and the shaping of destiny — on these let there be no faltering speech or lisp of hesitancy. "In my preaching," says Bunyan, "I have really been in pain, and have, as it were, travailed to bring forth children unto God; neither could I be satisfied unless some fruit did appear in my work. If I were fruitless it mattered not who commended me; but if I were fruitful I cared not who did condemn."

If I have not already trespassed too far on your patience I should like to say a word or two as to the way in which Bunyan seems to have realized the ideal minister, not only in his preaching, but also in the spirit of his life. I need not remind you how bravely and with what unshrinking fortitude he held on his way in spite of the storms and sorrows of life. Long weary years in gaol did not break his spirit or embitter his heart. "I have determined," said he, "the Almighty God being my help and shield, yet to suffer, if frail life might continue so long, even till the moss shall grow on mine eyebrows rather than to violate my faith and principles." In those days of persecution our fathers passed through stern discipline. Our sorrows are light indeed by the side of theirs. He had also troubles which every true minister of Christ has to share with him. He had heart-sorrows, as we have, too, over some who ran well once but were hindered. "If," said he, "any of those who were awakened by my ministry did after that fall back, as sometimes too many did, I can truly say their loss hath been more to me than if my own children, begotten of my own body, had been going to their graves. I think, verily, I may speak it without any offence to the Lord, nothing has gone so near to me as that, unless it was the fear of the loss of the salvation of my own soul."

Besides this sorrow, of which every minister knows something, he had experience of others also. He was bitterly assailed by evil men. The ignorant and malicious loaded him with slanders and reproaches. "What shall I say to those who have thus bespattered me?" asks he. "Shall I threaten them? Shall I chide them? Shall I flatter them? Shall I entreat them to hold their tongues? No, not I! I bind these things to me as an ornament; it belongs to my Christian profession to be vilified, slandered, reproached, and reviled. Wanting these I should want one sign of a Christian and child of God. I rejoice in reproaches for Christ's sake."

Judging, then, from other men's experience you are not to be surprised if in coming days you now and then meet with trouble and trying discipline in the exercise of your ministry. Indeed I know no walk of life where a man may altogether expect to escape, and I know no man who would be the better for it even if he could escape. We have to go through the deeps, both for our own sake and for the sake of others. We are to "comfort them that are in affliction through the comfort wherewith we ourselves are comforted of God." But I am not going to dwell too much on the shadows in the picture. For there is another and a brighter side. I believe that a man who has even moderate capacity for the work of the ministry, a love for his work and real Christlike sympathy with men, will in time gather about himself so much kind feeling from those he has helped, and who love him for his work's sake, that there may even be danger the other way. He may need to be saved from the enervating influence of too much kindness. Fortunately, if this should be your case, you may rely upon it that the Lord, in His mercy, will raise up some good brother in the church who will make it his business to see to it that you are not exalted above measure. My advice is that you should look upon that brother as one of your best friends. He has one talent at least, and though you may have preferred that he should have wrapped that one talent in a napkin and buried it in the earth, you may yet find that it has valuable uses.

In future years, then, you may have your trials and sorrows, no man is entirely without, but do not think too much of them; do not be always trying to run away from them to some other church — some church not yet created — where all is unbroken and unclouded peace. If you have your sorrows you will also have your joys; you will have meat to eat that the world knows not of. And the joys you will find to be most precious are not those which can be set forth in the religious journals of the day, but those you take to your secret place of communion, and spread before the Lord with a thankfulness too deep for words. If there are those you have helped to see the light of God, to bear their life-burdens, to go forward under hard conditions with new courage and hope — if there are those whom God has given you to be your children in the faith and whom you have the honor of building up to a noble Christian manhood, you will care very little for the troubles of the way. "I have," says Bunyan, "counted as if I had goodly buildings and lordships in those places where my children were born; my heart hath been so wrapped up in the glory of this excellent work that I counted myself more blessed and honored of God by this than if He had made me the Emperor of the Christian world, or the Lord of all the glory of the earth without it."

Bunyan's experience is interesting to us in another way, inasmuch as with all his genius he knew as much as most of us of those ups and downs, those exaltations and reactions of feeling of which every preacher, indeed every public speaker, knows the meaning. He had his temptations, he says, and that of divers kinds. Sometimes when he was on his way to preach he was haunted by a fear that he should not be able to speak to edification, nay that he should not be able even to speak sense to the people; at which times he would be seized with such strange faintness and strengthlessness of body that his legs would scarce carry him to the place of exercise. Sometimes, again, when he had begun to speak the word with much clearness, evidence and liberty of speech, before the opportunity was over he has become so straitened in speech and bewildered that he has not known what he has been about; or to use his own expression, he has felt as if his "head had been in a bag all the time of the exercise." Let this be your comfort if such experiences should ever be yours, and remember that the people have not always seen the sermon as you have yourself. Sometimes when you thought you have done well you have not done so well as you thought. On the other hand when you have felt humbled God has taken your weakness and filled it with his strength. "Sometimes," says Bunyan, "when I thought I did no good then I did most of all; and at other times, when I thought I should catch them, I have fished for nothing."

Like all true men, this man in his work felt he was nothing and God was everything. He knew his own heart too well ever to be proud or vainglorious. "I have also," he says, "while found in this blessed work of Christ, been often tempted to pride and liftings up of heart; and though I dare not say I have not been infected with this, yet truly the Lord of His precious mercy, hath so carried it towards me, that for the most part I have had but small joy to give way to such a thing. For it hath been my every day's portion to be let into the evil of my own heart, and still made to see such a multitude of corruptions and infirmities therein that it hath caused hanging down of the head under all my gifts and attainments. I have felt this thorn in the flesh the very mercy of God to me."

Thus this divinely-gifted and heaven-illumined soul was taught the great secret of spiritual strength; found out that the way to the heights is ever through the depths: that when we are weak then are we strong; and so with an ever-increasing sense of his own insufficiency came to feel more and more that his sufficiency was of God. Such pastors the churches need in every generation. From age to age they seem to say:

"We want *our* Bunyan to show the way
Through the Sloughs of Despond that are round us to-day,
Our guide for straggling souls to wait,
And lift the latch of the wicket-gate.
We fain would listen, O Preacher and Peer,
To a voice like that of this Tinker-Seer,
Who guided the Pilgrim up, beyond
The Valley of Death and the Slough of Despond,
And Doubting Castle and Giant Despair,
To those Delectable Mountains fair,
And over the River, and in at the Gate
Where for weary Pilgrims the Angels wait."

VI

RICHARD BAXTER, THE KIDDER-MINSTER PASTOR

LECTURE VI

RICHARD BAXTER, THE KIDDERMINSTER PASTOR

IN recent utterances of mine your attention has been called to certain English preachers of the seventeenth century who were, in an especial sense, characteristic of the time and notable in themselves. I should like, still, to detain you in that century a little while longer that we may receive further instruction and stimulus from the life-story of a distinguished preacher and the record of a memorable ministry which you will recognize as falling within the century I have named.

If I were asked what, in the year 1646, was one of the most unpromising towns in England to which a young man could be sent, who was starting his career as preacher and pastor, I should feel inclined to point at once to the town of Kidderminster in Worcestershire. With a population at that time of between three and four thousand, mainly carpet-weavers, it had been, morally and spiritually, so grossly neglected as almost to have sunk into practical heathenism. Few, indeed, were those in whose hearts any seeds of godliness had taken root. The majority of the people were ignorant beyond the ignorance of the time, debased beyond its defilement, disorderly beyond its rudeness. It was an illustration of the old adage — like priest like people. For the vicar of the town had been proceeded against before the Committee for Scandalous Ministers as being in character and attainments utterly unfit for his position. Ignorant of the very elements of Christianity, he preached but once a quarter, and that in so feeble a fashion as to expose him alike to the ridicule and the pity of the people who listened to him. It was also alleged against him that he was a frequenter of ale-houses, and had sometimes been seen drunk. Such was the vicar, and his curates were like himself. One of these was in the town, and, in common with his vicar, was accused before the Committee; the other had charge of a subordinate chapel in a distant part of the parish. This last was described as a common tippler and drunkard, as a railing quarreller, and an ignorant insufficient man who had scarcely knowledge enough to understand a Child's Catechism. Almost the only book he had was Musculus's "Commonplaces in English," out of which he used to string a few platitudes for the people; and the trade by which he chiefly lived was that of celebrating unlawful marriages. If the people strayed away to neighboring parishes they found themselves no better off. For the poor ignorant curate of the parish on the one side got his living by cutting fagots, and the curate of the parish on the other side by making ropes — "their abilities being answerable to their studies and employments." This was the condition in which scores of parishes were left after the best preachers had been driven by persecution either into Holland, or over here into New England. To undertake the pastoral care of a town like Kidderminster after such teachers as these was like undertaking to cultivate a farm which for time out of mind had been overrun with briars and thorns, and abandoned to thistles and weeds.

Again, if I were asked, who of all men — taking merely physical reasons into account — would seem to be the most unlikely man to be sent as pastor to this most unlikely and unpromising place, I should have said that man was Richard Baxter. Scarcely ever has a man who has done any work at all, done it under circumstances of such difficulty and pain as this man did his. For fourteen years he had scarcely a working hour free from pain. He was engaged in one long conflict with diseases like "pleurisy, nephritic and cholic." "I had at several times," he says, "the advice of no less than six and thirty physicians, by whose order I used drugs without number, almost all of which God thought not fit to make successful for a cure." Twenty several times he was near to death; again and again he was brought to the very gates of the grave, and again and again he returned to life through the long and wearisome ascent of slow and difficult recovery. If Richard Baxter had done nothing but take care of himself as an invalid, no one would have had the heart to blame a man to whom life was thus one long and weary battle with disease and pain.

And yet once more: If I were asked to single out one English town of the seventeenth century which more almost than any other came under the influence of the Spirit of God; and one preacher who, more than most, was successful in winning men for Christ, and in organizing a vigorous church life under his pastorate, I should say that town was Kidderminster and that preacher was Richard Baxter. A quarter of a century ago that town did honor to itself by erecting a statue to that preacher; and on the occasion of the unveiling, Dean Stanley said: "There have been three or four parishes in England which have been raised by their pastors to a national, almost a world-wide, fame. Of these the most conspicuous is Kidderminster: for Baxter without Kidderminster would have been but half of himself; and Kidderminster without Baxter would have had nothing but its carpets." Let us first look at the extent of the work this man did, and then at his methods of work.

With grateful heart he tells of the success God gave him in his ministry. And though the story is his own, we may safely trust him. There is an unmistakably honest ring about the man. "I would as soon doubt the Gospel verity," said Coleridge, "as I would doubt Baxter's veracity." "Let me," says he, "to the praise of my gracious Lord, acquaint you with some of my success." He will not suppress the story, though he knows beforehand that some will impute the mention of it to pride and ostentation, for it is the sacrifice of thanksgiving which he owes to his most gracious God, which he will not deny Him for fear of being censured as proud, lest he prove himself proud indeed.

He had not long been preaching in the town before the large and capacious church became so full that gallery after gallery had to be added to the interior. And as years went by the preaching in the church told powerfully upon the life of the town. Let him tell the wonderful story himself: "On the Lord's days there was no disorder to be seen in the streets, but you might hear a hundred families singing psalms and repeating sermons, as you passed through the streets. In a word, when I came thither first there was about one family in a street that worshipped God and called on his name; and when I came away there were some streets where there was not past one family in the side of a street that did not do so; and that did not by professing serious godliness give us hopes of their sincerity." The teaching in the church elevated those carpet-weavers intellectually as well as religiously: "Some of the poor men did competently understand the Body of Divinity, and were able to judge in difficult controversies." But, better still, they became gifted spiritually: "Some of them were so able in prayer that very few ministers did match them in order and fulness, and apt expressions and holy oratory with fervency." And, best of all, their lives were even better than their prayers: "The temper of their minds and the innocency of their lives was much more laudable than their parts. The professors of serious godliness were generally of very humble minds and carriage; of meek and quiet behavior unto others, and of blamelessness and innocency in their conversations." The sermons of the minister in the pulpit were preached over again by the people in their lives. They made the Gospel beautiful by showing it in action. Says Baxter: "The holy, humble, blameless lives of the religious sort was a great advantage to me: the malicious sort could not say—your professors here are as proud and covetous as any. But the blameless lives of godly people did shame opposers, and put to silence the ignorance of foolish men, and many were won by their good conversation." Moreover, this good work of God stood the test of time, was no mere flash in the pan. When the Restoration brought in the reign of persecution this true shepherd of men was driven from the people he loved so well, and who loved him; yet long afterwards he writes: "Though I have now been absent from them about six years, and they have been assaulted with pulpit calumnies and slanders, with threatenings and imprisonments, with enticing words and seducing reasonings, they yet stand fast and keep their integrity. Many of them are gone to God, and some are removed, and some now in prison, and most still at home; but not one that I hear of who has fallen off or forsaken his uprightness."

Now this is no mere ideal picture of some "sweet smiling" Auburn, with pastoral relations depicted after the fancy of the poet, but not easily to be met with in real life. It is a simple narrative of facts as they took place, not in some abode of rustic innocence, but in a manufacturing town where the weavers were often as busy with religious discussions as they were with their looms; where working-men have usually keen tongues, and are not over-sparing in their criticisms of preachers and sermons and churches. What is there to explain the exceptional success of this Kidderminster pastor?

That success certainly did not depend upon any mere adventitious aids. It did not lie with him in a comely presence, for he was weak and gaunt in form. He had no personal advantages except — and I must admit the exceptions I am about to name are not without significance — except that he had an eye which caught its fire from the ardor of his soul, and that he had as a natural gift a familiar moving voice, — a voice which a loving heart toned into the music of pathetic entreaty. A great analyst of the art of public speaking as it was brought to perfection in Greece said that a speaker must convince his hearers at the very outset: first, that he has their interests at heart, next, that he is competent to interpret these interests, and, thirdly, that he is free from the taint of self-seeking. It is scarcely likely that Richard Baxter gathered the precepts of the art of speaking from the great work of Aristotle, for Greek was not much in his way, but he certainly always had these purposes before him. He had that true genius for public speaking, that most effective form of eloquence which you see in a man when, in conversation on some serious subject, he is intent on convincing his neighbor of some important truth, or persuading him to some decisive course of conduct. Of public men in recent times in England, so far as I have had the opportunity of hearing them, I should say that John Bright had this true genius, this true oratorical instinct in the highest degree. The most cultured and intellectually-gifted men were conscious of an indescribable pleasure in listening to him when he was at his best, and the most studious and shrewd of the working classes made his speeches a household book. It is difficult to describe the style, but you recognize it at once, whether it is addressed to the eye or the ear. It is characterized by that brief, rapid, familiar and natural manner which a mind in earnest ever assumes. It shrinks instinctively from what is merely ornate or glittering. It is jealous of piled-up epithets, aims at a highly-idiomatic and homely diction, has a love of brevity and condensation, and keeps itself free from stiff stateliness and empty formality.

A competent witness in our time has expressed the opinion that of all the English preachers of the past, probably those who have been most strongly marked by the peculiarities of the true genius for public speaking are Hugh Latimer, Robert South and Richard Baxter. Of the quality of Hugh Latimer we had some taste in a former lecture. But South seems to this writer to furnish, in point of *style*, the truest specimen of the most effective species of pulpit eloquence. Of course he is speaking simply of his style, offering no opinion as to the truth or error of the doctrines he taught, and no apology for his unchristian bitterness and often unseemly wit. He merely points out that his robust intellect, his shrewd common sense, his vehement feelings, and his fancy, always more distinguished by force than by elegance, admirably qualified him to be a powerful public speaker. There is a sermon of his in which he pours scorn on the florid declamation, the mere tinsel rhetoric which some people think to be so very fine. He mentions no names, but you can see that he is speaking for the especial benefit of his illustrious but too fanciful and too ornate contemporary, Jeremy Taylor. The passage is worth quoting: "'I speak the words of soberness,' said St. Paul, and I preach the Gospel not 'with the enticing words of man's wisdom.' This was the way of the Apostle's discoursing of things sacred. Nothing here 'of the fringes of the north star;' nothing 'of nature's becoming unnatural;' nothing of the 'down of angels' wings, or the beautiful locks of cherubims;' no starched similitudes introduced with a 'Thus have I seen a cloud rolling in its airy mansion,' and the like. No—these were sublimities above the rise of the apostolic spirit. For the Apostles, poor mortals, were content to take lower steps, and to tell the world in plain terms that he who believed should be saved, and that he who believed not should be damned. And this was the dialect which pierced the conscience and made the hearers cry out, Men and brethren, what shall we do? It tickled not the ear, but it sunk into the heart, and when men came from such sermons they never commended the preacher for his taking voice or gesture; for the fineness of such a simile or the quaintness of such a sentence; but they spoke like men conquered with the overpowering force and evidence of the most concerning truths, much in the words of the two disciples going to Emmaus: 'Did not our hearts burn within us while He opened to us the Scriptures.'

In a word, the Apostles' preaching was therefore mighty and successful, because plain, natural and familiar, and by no means above the capacity of their hearers· nothing being more preposterous than for those who were professedly aiming at men's hearts, to miss the mark by shooting over their heads."

Passing from South to Baxter, we have in both, in large measure, those endowments essential to the best kind of popular eloquence. Baxter has the same combination of vigorous intellect and vehement speech which distinguished South; but he has what South had not, — a devotion pure and ethereal, a benevolence ardent and sincere. The vigorous, direct style of speech was inspired by the earnest soul. His weak health seemed always to keep him within sight of the things eternal. He says: "Doing all in bodily weakness, as a dying man, my soul was all the more easily brought to seriousness, and to preach as a dying man to dying men; for drowsy formality and customariness doth but stupefy the hearers and rock them asleep. It must be serious preaching which must make men serious in hearing and obeying it." The same earnestness of spirit is manifest in an appeal he makes to ministers themselves. "I confess," he says, "that NECESSITY should be the great disposer of a minister's course of study and labor. If we were sufficient for everything we might attempt everything, and take in order the whole Encyclopædia; but life is short, and we are dull, and eternal things are necessary, and the souls that depend on our teaching are precious. I confess, necessity hath been the conductor of my studies and life. It chooses what book I shall read, and tells me when and how long. It chooseth my text, and makes my sermon, both for matter and manner, so far as I can keep out my own corruption. Though I know the constant expectation of death hath been a great cause of this, yet I know no reason why the most healthy man should not make sure of the most necessary things first, considering the uncertainty and shortness of all men's lives."

This man's power, then, and the secret of his success lay in the natural human way he spoke to men, and the divine earnestness which possessed his soul. He spoke directly from Christ to the people. Christianity was to him no mere set of doctrines to be received or a code of ethics to be followed; it was the power of an endless life. Go and listen to him in that crowded church in Kidderminster any Sunday you like, he is the same man with the same theme. No one suspects that this soldier of the Cross fights uncertainly as one that beats the air. You feel that his message is not so much *about* his Master as *from* Him; and it is not a message that might do for any audience at any time, but it is clearly intended for the living men and women then and there before him. The minutes are not long enough for all he wants to say, and his most fervent words are not expressive enough to satisfy his eager soul. And even when he seems drawing to a close he is unwilling to turn and leave. He has yet one more argument, if, haply, one more soul may be persuaded. The people in those pews, listening, do not need to be told that the man who stands there speaking is not there merely because he has to go the round of his professional duties, but because in loyalty to God and his own soul he could be nowhere else. He feels and they know that he feels that necessity is laid upon him, yea, that woe is unto him if he preach not the Gospel. Like an apostle who went before him, he can truly say: I hold not my life of any account, as dear unto myself, so that I may accomplish my course, and the ministry which I received from the Lord Jesus, to testify the Gospel of the grace of God.

But Baxter's preaching, earnest and telling as it was, was not the only means he employed for the instruction of his people, and for the grounding of them in the truth. We have quickened the pace of life since his time, and manners and customs have greatly changed; but we may yet learn much from the business-like way in which he set about getting at the people. Once more we will let him tell the story himself:

"Every Thursday evening," he says, "my neighbors that were most desirous, and had opportunity, met at my house, and there one of them repeated the sermon, and afterwards they proposed what doubts had any of them had about the sermon, or any other case of conscience, and I resolved their doubts. And, last of all, I caused sometimes one and sometimes another of them to pray (to exercise them), and sometimes I prayed with them myself; which (besides singing a psalm) was all they did. And once a week, also, some of the younger sort, who were not fit to pray in so great an assembly, met among a few more privately, where they spent three hours in prayer together. Every Saturday night they met at some of their houses to repeat the sermon of the last Lord's day, and to pray and prepare themselves for the following day. Once in a few weeks we had a day of humiliation on one occasion or other. Two days every week my Assistant and I, myself, took fourteen families between us for private catechising and conference (he going through the parish and the town coming to me). I first heard them recite the words of the catechism, and then examined them about the sense, and, lastly, urged them with all possible engaging reason and vehemency to answerable affection and practice. If any of them were stalled through ignorance or bashfulness I forbore to press them any further to answers, but made them hearers, and either examined others or turned all into instruction and exhortation. I spent about an hour with a family, and admitted no others to be present, lest bashfulness should make it burthensome, or any should talk of the weaknesses of others. So that all the afternoons on Mondays and Tuesdays I spent in this (after I had begun it, for it was many years before I did attempt it); and my

Assistant spent the morning of the same days in the same employment."

Further on in his narrative Baxter adds: "When I set upon personal conference with each family, and catechising them, there were very few families in all the town that refused to come: and those few were beggars at the town's-ends, who were so ignorant that they were ashamed it should be manifest. And few families went from me without some tears, or seemingly serious promises for a godly life."

Truly this was a consecrated life. This man was not willing to go to heaven alone. Of him we may say, as Matthew Arnold said of his illustrious father: —

> "Thou wouldst not *alone*
> Be saved, my Father! *alone*
> Conquer and come to the goal,
> Leaving the rest in the wild. . . .
> Therefore to thee it was given
> Many to save with thyself;
> And at the end of thy day,
> O faithful Shepherd! to come
> Bringing thy sheep in thy hand."

The arrangements which Baxter tells us he carried out for coming into personal contact with his people suggest a subject of practical importance to the effective working of the Christian pastorate. His plans would scarcely fit in with the modes of modern life. The demands of business on the elders and of education on the juniors of the household, to say nothing of other aspects of the intense life of our time, make it difficult, if not impossible, to take family after family an hour at a time, two days in every week. Moreover, the engagements of public life on the part of the minister himself have multiplied to an extent of which our forefathers had but little experience. Still, after all such pleas have been listened to and duly weighed, it nevertheless remains true that for the effective working of our churches and the furthering of the kingdom of God among them it is of first importance for the minister to know the people and come into personal contact with them. And that not merely for social and friendly intercourse, which has its value, but also for direct spiritual purpose. Localities differ, and plans which succeed in one place may be inapplicable in another; but in every place the true-hearted minister of Christ will find some way of getting at his people and dealing with them with spiritual intent.

For one thing, it will give point and directness to his preaching. A minister can always preach to people to greater purpose when he knows them. This is the explanation of the fact that many of our best ministers preach better to their own people than they do anywhere else. You must know people if you would help them, and you must love them if you would know them. Love is the one power that opens the secrets of life, meets its reserves and calls forth its confidences. You can almost say anything to a man if he knows and feels that you really care for him and want to serve him. Sympathy, true heart-love for men, such as Christ manifested, will give clear insight, delicate touch and enduring patience in dealing with those under our care. It is twice blessed. It gives power to the minister and it is precious to the flock. There is enough sorrow in life, enough weakness and suffering, enough heart-yearning after better things to make men value the kindness which enters into their sorrow and would help them. The pastor may sometimes wonder why the people should care so much for his coming and for his entering into their experiences; but true brotherliness of soul will always be precious in a world like this, and will often do much to prepare the way of the Lord and make His paths straight.

And we may not only give much to others, but also gain much for ourselves. The sick-chamber, where saintly men and women face the realities of life and death alone with God, is a fine school for the minister. And even in the midst of the activities of life you meet with worthy Christian people who have gone through no university, taken no divinity course, who yet have been diligent scholars in the school of Christ, and are deeply learned in spiritual lore. It will be good for you to know them. You will feel nearer to heaven when you are near to them, will find your religious convictions intensified, and you will learn some inward truths which will qualify you more than ever to be the teacher of others. Inexperienced at starting, you will yet, in some sense, have to rule, and that, too, over the free minds of men educated in the freest of communities. You will need, therefore, to be a careful student of life and character. Both to teach well and to rule well you will need to know the living people about you. We who live so much with books need to be kept from the mistakes into which bookish men are only too apt to fall. The only way to keep clear of such mistakes is to come ever and again into contact with actual life.

In setting forth the causes of his success at Kidderminster, Baxter mentions one fact worthy of consideration. He says: "It much furthered my success that I stayed still in this one place (near two years before the wars, and above fourteen years after). For he that removeth oft from place to place may sow good seed in many places, but is not like to see much fruit in any; unless some other skilful hand shall follow him to water it. It was a great advantage to me to have almost all the religious people of the place of my own instructing and informing; and that they were not formed into erroneous and factious principles before; and that I stayed to see them grown up to some confirmedness and maturity." These seem to me wise words on the part of this preacher of the olden time. It is a pity when a minister comes under the dominion of what Bernard calls "a vagabond and unstable heart," for no unsettled life can truly thrive. When the learned Jeremiah Marsden, one of the ejected ministers, wrote godly meditations on his *twenty-second* removal, one does not wonder that he exclaimed: "O my soul, what a sojourning state hath thy life been! Now here, then there, and in no abiding posture!" And it is not surprising that he should express a longing to reach the city which hath foundations of God's laying. This is an exceptional case, of course, and occurred in troublous persecuting times. There is much to be gained by steadfast holding on so long as a man can do so with usefulness and hopefulness. If I may be pardoned a local and personal reference, I may mention that the church of which I have the honor to be minister lost its illustrious pastor, John Bunyan, by death, in 1688, that is, two hundred and eleven years ago, and I am only the sixth in succession since then, and all my predecessors remained in charge till death called them to the higher service; so that the average duration of these six pastorates is thirty-five years each. Well, I will say nothing of the present occupant of the pastorate, but of my predecessors I will say that they one and all acquired influence for good not only in their own congregation, but in the town at large, which they never would have had if, like some men, they had always been restlessly looking out for some other attractive sphere of service. Around them there gathered one of the most sacred possessions a minister can have — the loving affection of those who had grown up from childhood and youth to manhood by their side. No absolute rule can be laid down. There are times when a change may be best both for minister and people. Another place may call out powers in him which are only latent where he is, and another minister may do better work there than he is doing. Still I would say to you, with all brotherly affection when you leave the Divinity School of this University, to enter upon actual work, do not accept a charge with a reserved intention of finding a better when you can. No man can do justice to any people when he is always looking wistfully at the list of vacant churches and revolving a possible flight. Take the place meaning to do your best by it, as you are in honor bound to do. Do not make too much of your discouragements; do not let trifles shake your stability so long as you have the love of your people. Some of them may even leave you, but it is no disparagement to any minister that he does not suit every order of mind. God has many children, and they feed in different ways. "Therefore, my beloved brethren, be ye steadfast, unmovable, always abounding in the work of the Lord, forasmuch as ye know that your labor is not in vain in the Lord."

Up to this point I have been speaking of Baxter's preaching, his methods of work, and his persistence in the same sphere of service; I should like to say a word or two on the spirit of his life as a minister of Christ. There was a breadth of mind in the man not common in his day. He brought to the study of the Bible not only deep spiritual feeling, but also much independence of thought. His name is now a synonym for orthodoxy of belief, and he is held up as an example by those who bid us stand in the ways and see and ask for the old paths. It may surprise some people, therefore, to find that he was looked on with suspicion as heterodox, by the men of his own time. He was neither Calvinist nor Arminian, as these terms were understood then. The views he held on the theory of redemption were his own individual conclusions rather than the accepted formulas of some theological school. He would not deny a thing because it was incapable of demonstrative proof, nor reject seemingly opposite statements of Scripture because he could not reconcile them. He could neither agree with the ultra Calvinist nor with the violent Arminian; and though they both turned against him, they have each since then been approaching nearer and nearer the ground on which he took his stand. Whether we agree with his opinions or not we cannot but feel that he exercised a healthy influence on the Christian Church, that he initiated that opposition to extreme opinions which has been growing ever since, and that, as some one has said, his eclecticism was one of the first stones laid in that temple of theological unity which takes so many generations to build.

When past middle life Baxter wrote a kind of review of his earlier self, and of the ways he had of looking at things when he was younger, which is still fresh and racy to read. Dean Stanley tells us that Sir James Stephen once recommended him with his own peculiar solemnity to read the last twenty-four pages of the first part of Baxter's "Narrative of his own Life." "Lose not a day," said he, "in reading it. You will never repent of it." And says the Dean: "That very night I followed his advice, and

I have ever since publicly and privately advised every theological student to do the same." If at any time you should turn to those twenty-four pages in that old folio of 1696 you will feel that this praise is not ill-bestowed. There is in them the note of clear sanity of mind and the ring of honest sincerity of heart, and they show how we may all grow from less to more. He has learnt to be more tolerant, he says, as life has gone on. He sees that good men are not so good as he once thought them, and that few are so bad as their enemies imagine. In his youth he was quickly past fundamental questions and ran into a multitude of controversies. But the older he grew the smaller stress he laid upon these controversies and curiosities — though still his intellect abhorred confusion — as finding greater uncertainty in them and less usefulness where there is certainty. If he had any influence with younger men he would persuade them to study and live upon the essential doctrines of Christianity and godliness. He is going against the grain of the natural man in saying this: "I presume to say that in this I as much gainsay my natural inclination to subtility and accurateness in knowing, as they are likely to do by theirs, if they obey my counsel." He thinks that most controversies have more need of *right stating* than of *debating*, and that if his skill is increased in anything it is in separating the *real* from the *verbal*, and proving to the disputants that they differ less than they think they do. He has grown also more modest about himself: "Heretofore I knew much less than now, and yet was not half so much acquainted with my ignorance. I little knew how imperfectly I understood the points whose discovery delighted me, nor how many things I was yet a stranger to. But now I find far greater darkness upon all things, and perceive how very little it is that we know in comparison of that which we are ignorant of."

Coming to yet closer matters still, he has a deeper sense of sin than once he had. Once his sins troubled him, now it is his sinfulness. "In my younger years my trouble for sin was most about my actual failings in thought, word or action. But now I am much more troubled for *inward defects*, and omission or want of the vital duties or graces of the soul. Had I all the riches of the world how gladly would I give them for a fuller knowledge, belief and love of God and everlasting glory! These wants are the greatest burden of my life, which oft maketh my life itself a burden. To have sinned while I preached and wrote against sin, and had such abundant and great obligations from God, and made so many promises against it, doth lay me very low; not so much in fear of hell as in great displeasure against myself. When God forgiveth me I cannot forgive myself." But on the other hand, he has learnt to look less to himself and more to God: "Heretofore I placed much of my religion in tenderness of heart and grieving for sin and penitential tears; and less of it in the love of God, and studying His love and goodness, and in His joyful praises than now I do. And now I am less troubled for want of grief and tears — though I more value humility, and refuse not needed humiliation — but my conscience now looketh at Love and Delight in God and praising Him, as the top of all my religious duties, for which it is that I value and use the rest. . . . I was once wont to meditate most on my own heart, and to dwell at home, and look little higher; I was still poring either on my sins or wants or examining my sincerity. But now I see more need of a higher work; and that I should look oftener upon Christ and God and Heaven than upon my own heart. It is *above* that I must find matter of delight and joy and love and peace itself. Therefore I would have one thought *at home* upon myself and sins, and many thoughts *above* upon the high and amiable and beatifying Objects."

I have explained Baxter's marvellous success at Kidderminster by calling attention to his direct and powerful speech, his close contact with his people, and his going on steadily year after year urging men to come into the Kingdom of God. But may I not now say that all these things rested on something deeper still — that they gathered point, fire and force from the deep heart experiences revealed in the confessions I have read to you? This man got his power by being alone with God and by looking into the face of God! And it is there we must get power too. There is no substitute for this power and no other way of getting it. It is the soul that has caught fire from the altar which sets other souls on fire. Let me from Baxter's "Reformed Pastor" — which should be every pastor's companion — close with the burning words he addressed to his brethren in the ministry now more than two centuries ago. Speaking of the preacher's message as an ambassador for Christ, he says: "O the gravity, the seriousness, the incessant diligence which these things require! I know not what others think of them, but for my part I am ashamed of my stupidity, and wonder at myself that I deal not with my own and others' souls, as one that looks for the great day of the Lord; and that I can have room for almost any other thoughts or words, and that such astonishing matters do not wholly absorb my mind. I marvel how I can preach of them slightly and coldly; and how I can let men alone in their sins; and that I do not go to them, and beseech them, for the Lord's sake, to repent, however they take it, and whatever pains or trouble it should cost me! I seldom come out of the pulpit but my conscience smiteth me that I have been no more serious and fervent in such a case. It accuseth me not so much for want of ornaments or elegancy, nor for letting fall an unhandsome word; but it asketh me 'How couldst thou speak of life and death with such a heart? How couldst thou preach of heaven and hell in such a careless, sleepy manner? Dost thou believe what thou sayest? Art thou in earnest or in jest? Shouldst thou not weep over such a people, and should not thy tears interrupt thy words? Truly this is the peal that conscience doth ring in my ears. O Lord, do that on our own souls which Thou wouldst use us to do on the souls of others!"

VII

REPRESENTATIVE PREACHERS OF MODERN PURITANISM

I. THOMAS BINNEY AND C. H. SPURGEON

LECTURE VII

REPRESENTATIVE PREACHERS OF MODERN PURITANISM

I. THOMAS BINNEY AND C. H. SPURGEON

IN the last lecture we came under the spell of the devout and fervid spirit of Richard Baxter, a man it is good for every Christian minister to know. The literary form the Puritan sermon took in the seventeenth century may be unsuited to our time, but the spirit of the men who made Puritanism the force that it was and is, is a thing for all time. For many of them walked with God with a fervor of devotion and a closeness of fellowship all too rare in human life. The Two Thousand ejected from the ministry of the Church of England, for Nonconformity, in 1662, though cast out by man, were elect souls of God. Their unfaltering loyalty to conscience; the Christlike spirit in which they accepted the stern discipline of persecution, entailing the loss of liberty and home and means of livelihood; their subdued sorrow over enforced silent Sabbaths, and over separation from the flocks they had loved and served — all these things make them still a spiritual force, and their influence a possession for ever to the Church of God.

There were others of these men in those days, besides Richard Baxter, well worth our knowing. It is good for us still to commune in quiet hours with men like good Philip Henry, of Broad Oak in Shropshire, who hallowed all things by prayer; whose family life was sweet with a divine fragrance; and who lived in the spirit of that godly mother of his, who said, ere she left him, "My head is in heaven, and my heart is in heaven; it is but one step more and I shall be there too." We should find it helpful, also, to walk at times in loving converse with such saintly souls as Isaac Ambrose, the minister of Preston, who, not many miles from Standish village and Duxbury Hall, from which Miles Standish came, retired to quiet woods for meditative thought and wrestling prayer. Of this good man's communion with heaven we get such glimpses as these: "May 13: I retired to a solitary and silent place to practise especially the secret duties of a Christian;" "May 15: I fell on the duty of self-trial, and in the morning confessed my sins before and since conversion, wherein the Lord sweetly melted my heart." He found, as many have found, that the way to the heights is through the depths; for he says: "In the conclusion the Lord struck me with a reverence of His majesty and presence, filled my soul with spiritual refreshings, enlarged my heart with praises of Him and desires to live unto Him." So, again, not to dwell too long on these things, we feel how times have changed from restful repose to hasteful speed when we turn in with John Angier, the minister of Denton, in Lancashire. Born at Dedham, on our side the sea, his relatives founded the old church at Dedham, on your side; converted under the great Puritan preacher, John Rogers, trained at Emmanuel College, and continuing his preparation for the ministry under John Cotton, at Boston, he settled at Denton, where the spirit of his life seemed to diffuse the fragrance as of heaven itself. With his ministerial brethren from the neighborhood round he kept what were called "private days," for the purpose of deepening their own spiritual life, — days which were long remembered for the holy and solemn impressions produced upon the hearts of all. We feel we are but feeble folk in these days, when we find the great Nonconformist, Oliver Heywood, telling us how in the days of persecution, on one of these occasions in John Angier's house: "I continued about three hours in prayer, pouring out my soul before the Lord, principally on behalf of His church." This may be one extreme, but in this restless age we are perhaps in danger from the other, for it is the life which is lived with God which has power with men.

These men belonged to the heroic age of Nonconformity in England, and as they gradually passed away, unfortunately, they were not succeeded by men of the like kind. After the first quarter of the eighteenth century, and, indeed, during its course, a wave of lifeless Arian teaching passed over the pulpits of the land, and, as certainly as the night follows the day, slowly and insensibly there came a period of spiritual reaction and decline. Christless preaching is always followed by desolated sanctuaries and crumbling walls. First there came silence as to the great Evangelical truths so forcibly preached in an earlier time, — a silence which was explained at first as not arising from dislike to the old truths themselves, but only from dislike to the old modes of stating them. Definite teaching was objected to as dogmatism, and as being offensive and unprofitable. Stress came to be laid more on the natural and moral grounds of religion and less on the supernatural and spiritual. The old phrases still continued to be used, but they were emptied of their former meaning. It has been well said that both preachers and people continued to speak their fathers' language after they had lost their fathers' faith. There were many and honorable exceptions, of course; still, both in the Established Church and in the Nonconformist communities, the mere preaching of moral duties, apart from that grace of God in salvation by which alone they can be fulfilled, left the land mourning and desolate. The experiment of trying to make men better without the Cross of Christ for them and the Spirit of God within them was tried on as large a scale as it is ever likely to be tried again; and the result was a nation largely given over to coarseness and sensuality.

The awakening of religious life in the nation commenced when Wesley and Whitefield brought back the almost forgotten Gospel to the people. Men and women who had gone to sleep under the droning, drowsy preachers in the churches began to weep over their sins when there was brought to them the Gospel of God's love to us in Christ. And the revival among the people outside the churches told upon the life and preaching within. The Congregationalists received considerable accessions to their membership from among those converted under the fervid appeals of the field preachers. Still, even these churches, while retaining the Evangelic faith, looked somewhat doubtfully upon the revival movement. Respectability was dear to their hearts, and staid propriety sat in the chief seats of the synagogue. Many looked upon Wesley and Whitefield in those days very much as some people look upon the Salvation Army now; and Dr. Doddridge was censured by some of his brethren of the extremely proper sort for permitting George Whitefield to preach in his pulpit at Northampton. Even those ministers who had remained true to the Evangelic faith preached in set, formal manner, and in a rotund, rhetorical style which they had only too diligently imitated from Dr. Johnson, then regarded as the great master of style. It was Johnsonese without Johnson's vigor and point. One can only wonder now at the enduring patience of the good people who sat out some of the sermons of even some of the foremost men at the end of last century and the beginning of this. Samuel Palmer, for instance, the editor of the Nonconformist Memorial, was the successor of Matthew Henry at Hackney, and one of the predecessors of Thomas Binney at the Weigh House Church in London. He was also a considerable author and a preacher of influence in the city; yet as one reads his sermons now we fail to see how that influence was acquired. Platitude succeeds to platitude with dreary monotony. Some one has advised all preachers to avoid the *obvious*, but this man seems to ride across country in eager search of it. As an illustration let me give you the divisions of a sermon of his from the text: "And His commandments are not grievous." Referring to these commandments, "I shall apply," says he, "this commendation of them, and a high commendation indeed it is, which suggests a very cogent motive to obey them, the justice of which I shall now endeavor to evince by the mention of six particulars. Christ's commandments cannot be justly esteemed grievous, for (1) they are not unreasonable; (2) they are not impracticable; (3) they are not dishonorable; (4) they are not dangerous; (5) they are not unpleasant; and (6) they are not unprofitable." I think you will agree with me that the man in the pew who heard such a programme as that set forth in the pulpit, might well be pardoned if he either at once settled himself comfortably down to sleep or precipitately made for the door.[1]

In the early years of this century, as well as in the closing years of the century before, there were London preachers, really able men, and exercising wide influence as ministers, who were stiff and stately in their conduct of religious services, unreal and conventional past all bearing. A keen and not unkindly observer of the time has told us of a Congregational minister, south of the Thames, who sometimes had the honor of having even royal dukes in his congregation, and who in dignified manner employed a page to carry his sermon into the pulpit, arrange it carefully for his convenience on the cushion, and,

[1] Principal Caird was severe yet not far from the truth when he said that "the pattern sermon of the Georgian era seems to have been constructed almost expressly to steer clear of all possible ways of getting human beings to listen to it." — University Addresses, p. 201.

when the service was over, carry it safely back to him to his carriage. We are not surprised to be told that the preaching of this divine was especially attractive to people who did not wish to have their minds troubled with much thought nor their hearts excited with much feeling. His hearers were led along the path of easy description through green meadows, flowers blooming on every side. For them there were no rugged steeps to climb, neither were there any sublime outlooks over grand and distant scenes.

In this same first quarter of the present century a father and two sons occupied three of the most famous London pulpits, of whom it is said that they never forgot that they were "Reverend." One who knew them well tells us that all three alike were carefully precise, exact, regular, orthodox; never uttering a word they would wish to retract, or that would excite any feeling of suspicion or surprise in the minds of their hearers. Every text was treated as the orthodox commentators expounded it, every doctrine as the great divines proposed it. Calvin, Owen, Goodwin spoke through their lips, although they were not as learned as Calvin, nor so profound as Owen, nor so argumentative as

Goodwin. The introduction of each sermon consisted of four or five appropriate sentences. The divisions were carefully expressed and deliberately enunciated. They consisted of a like number of nouns, adjectives and verbs corresponding in their order and arrangement so as to be immediately apprehended and easily remembered. One division was never allowed to encroach upon the space appropriated to another. They were so perfectly arranged that there was no occasion to suppress a thought or to pass hastily over any part of the subject. All was exact, precise, regular, just as propriety required, and as the hearers expected. The preacher knew exactly when to finish, and just as exactly his hearers knew when to expect the concluding sentences.

This regular round of staid propriety and kid-gloved gentility had gone on so long, year after year, that it had almost come to be looked upon as part of the system of the universe. Happily, however, in the earlier half of the present century there came a change to a broader and more living spirit in the churches. Indeed, the spirit of change was abroad in many departments of human thought before that. A wave of feeling passed over Europe after a time of stagnation. We see it in poetry as well as in political life. The ruling spirits in English Poetry, previous to 1770, were Dryden, Pope, Swift, Prior, and men of their school who, while maintaining that "the proper study of mankind is man," approached that study from the side of cold speculation and with the pen of satire. After a pause Cowper appeared with his "Task," bringing a kindlier and truer spirit; teaching men to love Nature for her own sake, and to sympathize with human life irrespective of caste and convention. Three years later came Burns, with his earlier poems, restoring that passion to our poetry which it had lost since the days of Elizabeth. The way having thus been prepared for him, Wordsworth appeared, looking at Nature lovingly and at man's life sympathetically; he, in his turn, again preparing the way for Tennyson and the rest who were to follow. The change accomplished was nothing short of a revolution.

Not merely in politics and in poetry, but still more in religious life and thought we seem to pass from one world to another when we pass from the eighteenth century to the nineteenth. The Puritan theology of the

Congregational churches had been modified by the great Evangelical revival, and also by the necessity of conflict, long continued, with Arian and Socinian teaching. The revival, bringing a new wave of spiritual influence over the churches, created new spiritual activities. Missionary societies were organized, a Bible society was formed, and a craving came over Christian men for more brotherly communion and greater unity in service than they had known before. It was impossible that the pulpit should remain untouched by the combined force of these various waves of influence. Of necessity it caught the freer inspiration of this new birth-time, and to some extent broke away from the stiff conventionality, the formal precision, and the wearisome wordiness which had too long cramped its message and its life. It is to this Renaissance of Preaching which came into the modern Puritanism of England I wish to invite your attention now. We will look at it in the persons of some of its characteristic representatives.

During the first quarter of the present century the pulpit of one of the foremost Congregational churches in the city of London was occupied by John Clayton, perhaps the most conspicuous of the formal, precise and genteel ministers I have described to you. He had a wealthy congregation to which he ministered for more than forty years; and his all-too-complacent biographer tells us, with a little flutter of delight, how, at the close of every service, there might be seen at the door of his church "from sixteen to twenty equipages, or full-appointed gentlemen's carriages, waiting to convey their owners, after service, to suburban villages." For years and years this ministry went on; but at length, like all things earthly, it came to an end at last, and with it, so far as that church was concerned, "the age of silk and lavender, and of successful suppression of thought under decorous phrases, came to an end," also. Then, in 1829, like a breeze from the hills, there came to the vacant pulpit a preacher who was every inch a man, and who cared very little indeed for "equipages or full-appointed gentlemen's carriages." This preacher was that Thomas Binney whom, as I have already told you, Alexander Maclaren described as "the man who taught me to preach."

This new celebrity had been quietly maturing for five years in the seclusion of an obscure pastorate in the Isle of Wight. Though not physically robust in those days, he was yet a striking personality, tall, erect, commanding, one of Nature's aristocracy — a born king of men. We may say of him as Calamy said of John Howe: "There is that in his looks and carriage which discovers that he has something within him which is uncommonly great and tends to excite veneration." It would be exaggeration to say that this man, by himself, ushered in a new era; for, as we have seen, it was a time of national upwaking in many directions. It would be true, however, to say that so far as the Congregationalists of England were concerned, he was the foremost and strongest of those who delivered the pulpit from artificially-constructed sermons and stilted rhetoric, and began to speak to men from the preacher's desk in human, familiar, everyday speech.

Speaking generally, the preaching before his time largely consisted of ethical disquisitions or abstract discussions of Christian doctrine. In a style which at once arrested attention, Mr. Binney sought to bring God's revelation in Scripture and man's life into vital and fruitful relations, and to make the one interpret the other. To him the spiritual universe as revealed in the Scriptures, and unfolded in the Christian experience of the Church, was as real as the natural world is to the man of science; and in scientific manner he investigated the laws of that universe, applied its facts and verified his conclusions by the facts. To him the Scripture was a living and authoritative word from God, declaring not speculations but divine facts, and revealing divine forces which, like the leaves of the Tree of Life, were for the healing of the nations. He was not himself, he would not have any Christian minister to be, the merely cloistered student, immersed in books, and knowing but little of the ways of men. On one occasion when addressing some divinity students, he said to them: "As you walk through the streets, having prayed in the study, keep your eyes open there; look at all things, prices and people, how they buy and how they sell, the sellers and the purchasers, the hours of labor and the hours of rest; try to look at all, try to know the whole tariff of trade, and do not be afraid to find in it all matter for your sermons. You are to be teachers — commend yourselves to every man's conscience in the sight of God. Know the world's thoughts and the world's ways, that you may be the world's masters and ministers."

But while thus conversant with actual life himself, as he would have all preachers to be, the great purpose of Mr. Binney's ministry was to make vital to the people the Scriptures of God. From the first he was recognized by the men of his own time as a lineal descendant of the men of Puritan days. His great sermons were treatises after the old Puritan plan as regards extent of discussion; but that discussion was carried on with such freshness and vividness that the old familiar truths were clothed with new and living power. I may instance, for example, the Annual Missionary Sermon he preached in the May of 1839. It was an occasion which, year by year, was counted great and drew memorable audiences. In the year I have mentioned, Mr. Binney was the preacher, taking for his subject: "Messiah Suffering and Messiah Satisfied" (Isa. liii. 11). One who heard him that day tells us that for nearly two hours he enchained the attention of that vast audience by the force of his arguments and the fervor of his appeals — fire flashing out sentence after sentence; electric life, as it were, flowing not only from his lips, but from face and form, from look and gesture, in short, from the whole man. And while thus remarkable for sermons of great massiveness and force, of rich imagination and highly-cultured beauty; and while able to enthrall for hours one of the most representative audiences of thoughtful men, he could also keep his hold on simple village folk quite as effectively as on the most cultured congregation. One who went with him says that he could never forget a sermon he heard him preach in a little country chapel from the text: "The Lord God is a sun and shield." His audience might number between one and two hundred, and there he stood talking familiarly, but with singular wisdom and beauty, on the light and defence which the Lord God is to His people. He gathered fitting illustration from the sunshine pouring that summer's day through the windows of the ivy-mantled walls; and then, comparing Jehovah to a shield of strength, a tower of protection, he spoke of the believer as a child within the impregnable fortress of his father, and looking, without fear, upon foes assailing its gates.

You will probably gather, from what I

have said, that this preacher did not read his sermons. As a rule he did not even write them, although after thinking them out, he carefully, by writing, prepared them for speaking. He admitted that reading has its advantages, and in an early book of his even advocated that mode of preaching, contending that there is no reason why a written composition should be tame or its delivery inanimate. For with a view to oral delivery the sermon may be written with freedom and force, with vigorous images and fervid declamation; it may be composed for the hearing of numbers and delivered with the earnestness of nature, sincerity, and zeal. Still, these expressed opinions of his earlier time notwithstanding, except on very rare occasions, Mr. Binney did not read his sermons. If he had done so he certainly would not have been the preacher he was. Reading, no doubt, secures self-possession, but sometimes self-abandonment is more powerful than self-possession. The preacher's eye fixed on his paper is missed by the people, and the grander swell of the soul is missed also. When a man is master of his subject he can watch the effect of his words on his audience, can contract or expand his arguments and vary his illustrations according as he sees that he is holding or not holding his audience. Some of the happiest flights of a preacher are those which are born of the occasion, the success of which goes far to atone for any defects of style there may happen to be. The whole history of preaching revivals points in the same direction. The appeal has always been from the scribes to the teacher who seems to speak with authority. "I like that man," said a Canadian trapper after hearing a certain preacher. "He 's the first preacher I 've ever met who could shoot without a rest." This man's illustration was drawn from the line of his own experience. The trapper who required a rest for his gun before he could fire would probably not carry home much game at nightfall.

Be that as it may, and while every man will determine for himself on this point, Mr. Binney's greatest triumphs in the pulpit were those of free speech. Generally speaking, without a note and with characteristic attitude, the forefinger of the right hand now and again laid upon the palm of his left, he made his way along the path he had previously intended to travel. Sometimes, for a moment, he would seem to hesitate or deliberate, as if casting about for the best way of marshalling his arguments or presenting his thoughts; at other times he rose on the swell of some great utterance or inspiring truth, and having gained some lofty eminence would step back and look round upon his audience as if to see how far he was carrying them with him. He has been described as a great master of *accent* in speech. While some men run their words along like engines on a line of rail, by *accent* of voice and hand, which has entrance into soul, he carried his people with him, and threw in tender effects which, without any mere artifice of emotion, would sometimes melt men to tears. Great in delineations of character, he made the men and women of Scripture story live and move before you. He seemed to carry his audience to the very heart of things, compelled them to listen, and made them feel that he was dealing with their deepest, truest life. The moral earnestness with which his preaching was charged showed itself in the subjects he chose, the manner of their treatment, and the way he brought them home to the hearts and lives of men; and his appeals gathered into themselves all the potent elements of the sermon by which they were preceded.

One thing specially noticeable about Mr. Binney's ministry was the devout and elevated spirit which marked the prayers of the sanctuary. Someone described him as "a devotional man talking intellectually." The author of the "Life of Chatterton," himself a poet and critic, once turned in to hear this preacher in his early London days, and he tells us he was as much struck with the prayers as with the sermon. "The prayer," he says, "which succeeds the reading of the chapter in the Bible is eminently devotional. The voice of the minister is deep and solemn, and his manner that of one who feels how infinitely great is He with whom he has to do. There is no familiarity, no bawling, no hurry; all is calmness, earnestness, and quiet supplication." Mr. Binney laid great stress on the importance of this part of the service, and his people felt, many a time, that he seemed to carry them in prayer to the very gates of heaven. Extempore prayer may sometimes suffer from the distempered mood of the minister, but it also gains by embodying the highest inspirations of the Spirit of God.

Let me now pass from one who was among the earliest to bring a living spirit into the

English pulpit of the nineteenth century, to set before you a representative of modern Puritanism, who was certainly one of the most striking personalities of the century, and who, by the sheer force of his own individuality made a conspicuous place for himself among the preachers of the time. I refer to the late Mr. Spurgeon. He was, what Mr. Binney was not, a popular preacher, followed from first to last by thousands. The common people, as usual, came first, but while they remained they were soon joined by men of higher social grade. Professional men, senatorial men, ministers of State and peers of the realm were to be seen among his audience. On the other hand, some of the cultured heathen assailed him relentlessly. The weekly journal which John Bright described as "the great Saturday Reviler," made him the perpetual butt of jibe and jeer. He simply smiled and said: "Give me the love of God and the hatred of the 'Saturday Review,' and I shall be sure to succeed." So he went on his way, proving, beyond a doubt, that no one can write a man down but himself.

It would be interesting to inquire what is the secret of a success, admittedly well deserved, and certainly unparalleled in England since the days of Whitefield and Wesley. Mr. Spurgeon's ecclesiastical relationships cannot account for it, for he began his ministry in London in an obscure place of worship belonging to one of the straitest and narrowest of Baptist sects; and the congregation to which he went had dwindled almost to the point of extinction. Then, too, so far as the man himself was concerned, there was nothing about his personal appearance to account for his success. His face, it is true, could light up wonderfully when he was fairly under weigh; but when he first stepped to the front of his vast audience his appearance was that of a man, short, stout, commonplace, and perfectly innocent of the æsthetics of dress. While his face, of round, homely Saxon cast, indicated a rude strength of purpose, and dogged power of endurance, it gave scant sign indeed of high intellectual expression. Further, he owed nothing to systematic academic training. He was by no means an ignorant man; for he had been an usher in a school, knew something of Latin and French, and had diligently made the most of his opportunities. Still those opportunities had been scanty enough. In metaphysics and theology his mind was in a somewhat crude condition, and his lack of acquaintance with the original languages of the Scriptures sometimes led to havoc in his exegesis. A public man who went to hear him in his early days attributed much of his popularity to his remarkable voice, and prophesied that so long as that voice lasted the popularity would last. Yet, from all one hears, Whitefield's voice must have been immeasurably superior in point of compass and richness. Mr. Spurgeon's was a comparatively level voice, its principal attributes being distinctness and force. It took a clear, sound, bell-like ring along with it, but it had few rich notes either of loftiness or tenderness. After all, the mere fact that ten thousand people could hear him when he spoke does not explain how he came to attract ten thousand people to hear him speak.

The explanation is to be sought elsewhere. And, first of all, it is largely to be found in the fact that his way of speaking to men was so perfectly natural. There was pathos and humor in him, as men have when they talk together in private life, and his preaching was as when one man is talking with his neighbor. No pulpit twang had he, none of the wearisome sing-song by which some preachers generate clerical sore-throat. He was as natural in the pulpit as John Bright was on the platform, and often more racy. He was what the common people call a born preacher; his mind readily taking in all he saw and heard and read, giving it out again with fulness and freshness, and without a faltering word.

Coming to the style of the man, there was nothing hackneyed about it even when he took a commonplace subject. If there is one thought more hackneyed than another by moralists and preachers it is perhaps that of the flight of time. But see how this man handles it: "Only a few Sabbaths ago," says he, "I was talking to you of Ruth in the harvest-fields, and of the heavily-laden wagon that was pressed down with sheaves; and now the leaves are almost gone; but few remain upon the trees; these frosty nights and strong winds have swept the giants of the forest till their limbs are bare, and the hoar frosts plate them with silver. Then, before we shall have time to burn the winter's log, we shall see the snowdrops and the yellow crocus heralding another spring! At what a rate we whirl along! Childhood seems to travel in a wagon, but manhood at express speed." There is nothing hackneyed or stilted about that. So, again, with his illustrations. Listen to this: "Have you ever read Coleridge's 'Ancient Mariner'?" asks he. "I dare say you have thought it one of the strangest imaginations ever put together, especially that part where the old mariner represents the corpses of all the dead men rising up — all of them dead, yet rising up to manage the ship; dead men pulling the ropes, dead men steering, dead men spreading the sails. I thought what a strange idea that was. But do you know I have lived to see that true: I have seen it done. I have gone into churches, and I have seen a dead man in the pulpit, and a dead man as a deacon, and a dead man holding the plate at the door, and dead men sitting to hear. 'No!' says one, 'you cannot mean it.' Yes, I do; the men were spiritually dead. I have seen the minister preaching, without a particle of life, a sermon which is only fresh in the sense in which a fish is fresh when it has been packed in ice. I have seen the people sit, and they have listened as if they had been a group of statues — the chiselled marble would have been as much affected by the sermon as they. I have seen the deacons go about their business just as orderly, and with as much precision as if they had been mere automatons, and not men with hearts and souls at all. Do you think God will ever bless a church like that? Are we ever to take the kingdom of heaven with a troop of dead men? Never! We want living ministers, living hearers, living deacons, living elders; and until we have such men who have got the very fire of life burning in their souls, who have got tongues of life and eyes of life, and souls of life, we shall never see the kingdom of heaven taken by storm. 'For the kingdom of heaven suffereth violence, and the violent take it by force.'"

Another important element in Mr. Spurgeon's success lay in the fact that he was a speaker of superb English: a master of that Saxon speech which somehow goes warm to the hearts of men. While the common people followed him in crowds, and heard him gladly, he had no more delighted listener or warmer personal friend than John Ruskin, the great master of a glowing and gorgeous English style. More than any man I know of in this century, he has shown us what a powerful weapon noble English speech may be when a man knows how to use it. Because of this he is worthy of prolonged and careful study on the part of every preacher. He had this much-to-be-desired power of racy English by native endowment, no doubt. He had it when he first opened his lips to speak to simple village folk in the fen-lands of Cambridgeshire. But, also, it is to be noted that the power grew — grew by deepening acquaintance with the writings of men conspicuous for the strength and grandeur of their English style. Like John Bunyan, he gained both the grandeur and the simplicity of his English prose from his English Bible; and also by being much in company with writers like Bunyan. There is something here worthy of every preacher's heedful care. The great classics of Greece and Rome must ever remain among our foremost instruments of intellectual culture; at the same time a broad-minded and careful study of our own best English writers must be among the first duties of him who would be a pleader with men in their English tongue.

It is but scant space I have left myself in which to speak of one other element in Mr. Spurgeon's success, as a preacher of Christ's Gospel, without which, I venture to think, in spite of his great gifts, he would not have done the work he did. It is that there was profound truth in the great substance of his teaching, and he himself believed that truth with all his heart. His message embraced the great Catholic truths of the Gospel — the yearning love of God for men, sinful as they are; the Incarnation of the Son of God; the Atonement for sin made by Christ's sacrificial death upon the cross; the influence of the Holy Spirit in the conversion and upbuilding of the human soul. All these truths and those which spring out of them he held with an unwavering grasp. No one could make him believe that the age of the supernatural had passed; for he boldly declared that the Gospel comes from the supernatural, *is* supernatural, and does its appointed work in the presence and by the power of the supernatural. On all these subjects his mind was made up past all misgiving. Forty years ago a reviewer, who was not insensible to such defects as Mr. Spurgeon certainly had, especially in the early years of his career, wrote what may still be repeated after these forty years have come and gone: "The philosophical precision, the literary refinements, the nice discriminations between what we may know of a doctrine, and what we may not, leaving us, in the end, perhaps scarcely anything to know about — all this, which, according to some, is so much needed by the age, is Mr. Spurgeon's utter scorn. He is the direct dogmatic enunciator of the old Pauline truth, without the slightest attempt to soften its outline, its substance, or its results — and what has followed? Truly, Providence would seem once more to have made foolish the wisdom of this world. While the gentlemen who know so well how people ought to preach are left to exemplify their profound lessons before empty benches and in obscure corners, this young man can point to six thousand hearers every Sunday, and ask — Who, with such a sight before him, dares despair of making the Gospel — the good old Gospel — a power in the great heart of humanity?"

VIII

REPRESENTATIVE PREACHERS OF MODERN PURITANISM

II. DR. R. W. DALE

LECTURE VIII

REPRESENTATIVE PREACHERS OF MODERN PURITANISM

II. DR. R. W. DALE

IN my last lecture I called your attention to two men who may be regarded as typical representatives of the English Puritan preacher of the nineteenth century, — Thomas Binney and Charles Haddon Spurgeon. I pass now from these to the late Dr. Dale of Birmingham, a preacher of whom a competent witness has said that "he had the real soul of the Puritan in him," and that as a theologian "our generation has had no abler interpreter of Evangelical thought." We may go one step farther and say that not merely this generation but this century has seen no abler man in the ranks of the English Congregational Ministry.

It is not necessary for me, here and now, to explain Dr. Dale's methods of work as a preacher, inasmuch as some years ago, as a former Yale lecturer, he practically did this for himself. Upon his characteristic qualities as a man and a minister I therefore do not propose to dwell. But Dr. Dale was not merely a preacher; he was also an independent and constructive theologian, which, it is scarcely necessary to say, all preachers are not. As the foundation of his preaching, there was a strong, compact, and solid basis of theological thought which gave real unity to all his teaching. With sweat of brain and earnest wrestling of soul he wrought out for himself, from divine revelation, a doctrinal system, which he sought to verify at every step by his own actual religious experience and by that of the Christian Church at large. One who had exceptional means of knowing him tells us that "he thought himself into the mind of the sacred writers, taking his first principle from John, and working it into a theology by means of terms and processes he derived from Paul, so that his theological method was at once Biblical and constructive."

The important place which theological study should hold in a preacher's life and teaching was emphasized early by Dr. Dale in what has always seemed to me to be one of the greatest of his sermons, that which he preached at Stratford-on-Avon in 1864, on the occasion of the tercentenary celebration of Shakespeare's birth. The sermon is entitled "Genius the Gift of God." In eloquent terms he spoke of the magnitude of the blessing God conferred on the English people when he endowed their great poet with gifts so vast and so rare; and also of how much that poet had done to give to the English tongue its force, its picturesqueness, its majesty, splendor, and beauty. But all this genius he seemed almost to covet for still higher service. He had sometimes tried, he said, to imagine what would have been the preciousness of that legacy which Shakespeare would have left to the world had his genius been wholly devoted to illustrate and enforce religious truth. He maintained that the highest ministry of all in which the intellect can be engaged, the ministry to which by its divine origin it is most urgently and imperatively called, is in direct connection with religion. He held it a crime against God and man to relegate the intellect to inferior provinces of thought and to forbid or discourage its activity in the investigation and mastery of religious truth. For it is in the revelation of God to man that the human mind finds the grandest materials for the exercise of its energy. It seemed to him that the vague uncertainty of theological thought with which some men ask us to be satisfied is virtually to cast dishonor on the dignity of human nature and to impeach the sincerity of divine revelation. He returned to this point towards the end of his life, and in a letter to a friend said that for years he had felt that the vagueness of thought which prevails among intelligent people with regard to Christian doctrine is a serious injury to the vigor of religious life; and that the injury was all the graver because of the increasing precision with which men are thinking about natural phenomena. In one region of the intellectual life there is granite, above it are clouds.

There are those who are afraid of dogmatic theology. Dogma is a word that scares them. Abusive epithets are so continually being applied to it that they think they show culture and breadth of mind by keeping clear of it. Yet what is dogma, rightly looked at, but the way a sensible man has of summing up his knowledge on a given subject? The necessity for dogma arises from that other necessity there is in the human mind for constructive movement and systematic thought.

There must be some sort of order in the way different parts of a subject hang together in the mind of an active thinker. Therefore, just as there may be a true and constructive science of the material universe, there may also be a true and constructive dogmatic theology, that is, a science of the spiritual universe. Neither in the one case nor the other may that science be perfectly complete and absolutely final. Natural science is continually seeking to adjust itself more and more closely to the facts; it is therefore no disparagement to spiritual science, that is, dogmatic theology, to say that it may have to do the same. The facts in both worlds, natural and spiritual, remain ever the same, unchanged and unchangeable, but man's way of expressing them and setting them forth must necessarily change as his knowledge of those facts becomes closer and more accurate. The spiritual world with its divine facts, laws, and processes is as real as the natural world, indeed the two are forever interlacing, and if the scientific study of the natural world is a high and honorable pursuit, so also is the scientific study of the spiritual. As men who desire to take life seriously, we must give some account of spiritual facts to ourselves and to others. There must be an intellectual expression of the contents of faith.

Possibly some men reject dogma because they dislike the facts with which dogma deals, but also very much of the opprobrium heaped upon it arises from the attempt too often made to stereotype in creeds for all time, the way some men had of expressing divine facts at some one given time. The attempt to stereotype natural science would not succeed. It would be very unfortunate if it did. So with the science of the spiritual universe. While its facts abide and are eternal, the form of stating them has changed, and indeed must change, if it is to have life in it and be of any value. The intellectual methods of the Middle Ages, as Dr. Dale points out, governed the speculations of the Schoolmen as to the invisible and spiritual universe just as they governed the speculations of their contemporaries in their researches into the visible and material universe. And in the interests of advancing knowledge those methods had to be left behind. So again, the Protestant attempt to recast theological thought after the Reformation, while substantially sound and strong, has undergone change and modification as the spiritual consciousness of the Church in communion with God has entered more fully into the spiritual heritage of truth. The men of thirty and forty years ago who urged us to be faithful to the theology of the Puritans were hardly conscious how far they themselves had travelled from the Puritan position. Mr. Spurgeon flattered himself to the end of his life that he was a sound Calvinist, yet John Calvin was much too great a theologian to have accepted Mr. Spurgeon's way of preaching Calvinism. As the Schoolmen of the Middle Ages, and the Protestants and Puritans of the sixteenth and seventeenth centuries thought and spoke in the idiom of their own time, Dr. Dale contended so must we. We in our turn have to give our own account of the great objects of faith, to construct our own conception of them, to conceive of them according to our own intellectual methods, and under our own forms of thought. We may not for a moment let go any of the divine facts or truths revealed to us. We dare not modify any traditional Christian doctrine to conciliate hostility. But neither are we to shrink from modifying any expression or tradition of the past which misrepresents the eternal fact. A recent writer has forcibly said that the right thing to do with dogma is not to *reject* it but to *vitalize* it. "It is a poor thing," he says, for example, "to preach 'Predestination' in such a way as to set men wondering whether they are predestinated or not, and which of their neighbors are. A man who inquires so is not predestinated very much. What we need is to put men in direct contact with Divine Power and Reality, to make life so serious to them that they will have the feeling which first made men throw out this word 'Predestination'—the feeling that they are arrested for a divine purpose, and must do a divine work. Predestination is man interpreting the 'must' of his inner nature as the eternal word and will of God."

Dr. Dale not only felt it needful to work out a system of Christian doctrine for his own intellectual and spiritual requirements, but he held it to be a foremost part of his duty to preach sermons on Christian doctrine to his people. In the preface to the latest book he himself issued from the press, he tells us that early in his ministry some other minister, in friendly fashion, said to him, "I hear that you are preaching doctrinal sermons to your congregation; they will not stand it." To which he replied, "They will have to stand it." Commenting upon this late in life, he admitted there was too much of the insolent self-confidence of youth in both the temper and form of his reply; at the same time he still held that the conception of the ministry which it expressed was a just one — as far as it went; and it was a conception which with more or less fidelity he had endeavored to fulfil. But while it is true that Dr. Dale felt it to be his duty to preach doctrinal sermons to a miscellaneous congregation, it is important to remember, what Dr. Fairbairn points out, that he never could regard a doctrine as a dogma which he was bound to believe because the Church had formulated it. Doctrine, while shaping his experience, was also verified by the experience which it governed. It may be asked, however, Is it competent for any man to limit divine truth within the bounds of his own experience? Is not this to resolve Christianity into mere subjective feeling? This, as Herrmann saw, was the vice of mysticism, that it disregarded the link between the inner life of the Christian and its real foundation in that which is outside itself, and so came to allow feelings which have no distinct character to usurp the place of thoughts concerning faith. Pietism, by disparaging intellectual activity, as Dr. Dale himself plainly saw, encourages a feeble religious sentimentalism. He was saved from that not only because, as Dr. Fairbairn says, his nature was large and rich, but because he was strongly intellectual, with a reason that was more ratiocinative than speculative. There was, to quote the far-seeing words of Herrmann, a further and more important safeguard: "The new state of feeling into which the Christian enters clings to something richer than itself. It needs an objective reality which it distinguishes from its own nature. Greater and higher than all religious emotion within the Christian, there rises and towers religious thought, which points away beyond all that we have already felt and experienced on to a boundless wealth which lies beyond." Thus while experience illumined and made real the truth of revelation, that truth guided and enriched the experience. Out of mutual interaction came enlargement of thought and life.

From what I have said, you will have gathered that Dr. Dale made it his habit to preach doctrinal sermons, in turns with sermons of other sort, because he held it to be his first and foremost duty to instruct his people as to those great divine facts of the spiritual universe which have been revealed to us. He felt it was not enough to give mere ethical teaching on the daily conduct of life. He did this, did it more effectively than most preachers, as his published sermons remain to shew. But he realized that eternity was the solemn background of time, and that no life is truly noble till it is rooted in divine relationships.

But while setting forth the great doctrines of revelation in his regular ministry, he did so in no merely technical or academic fashion. He made doctrinal preaching living by bringing it into close connection with, and verifying it by, the actual experience of living men. This is the one instructive thing about it for other preachers. Let me, in the briefest possible way, give instances of this.

For example, while proclaiming the foundation truth of the Divine Existence, he explained the difference between *believing* that God is, and *knowing* that He is. The *belief* may come from parents and teachers or as a national tradition. We *know* that God is by coming into personal contact with Him. One man remembers a summer's day when the wonderful beauty of nature filled him with exultation and delight. Suddenly through all that he saw there came the very glory of God. He knew that He was there. His presence and His goodness took possession of him and held him for hours. Another man comes to the same knowledge by finding an intelligible order in nature, by recognizing a mind not his, but like his, by finding that he can think God's thoughts after Him. Not by reasoning, but by experience is God's existence made certain to us. As the material world is perceived and known by the organs of sense, so God is perceived and known by the organs of the mind. The World, Self, God, — these are the ultimate realities; and each must be known by experience, if known at all. So again with the moral sense. When a man has done wrong, in the remorse and wretchedness which follow he has to do not with a mere idea, but with an awful force. It is more than a Power. It deals with him as a living Person deals with a living person. Righteousness is the attribute of a Person not of a mere Power; the Power which insists on Righteousness must have a living Person behind it. God has come to him, — the Living God. He knows there is a God; he knows it for himself.

But more commonly the traditional belief

in God's existence passes into the immediate and certain knowledge of Him under the power of the Christian Gospel, and the manifestation of the divine glory in the earthly history of our Lord Jesus Christ. A man becomes conscious of failure, or in other ways is led to the supreme life. There follows the great venture of faith. A cry goes up to God from the very depths of the soul, a cry of faltering trust and hope. The cry is answered, sometimes suddenly, sometimes after long delay. But whether earlier or later, the answer comes; and the man knows that it comes from the Living God. The faith of the Church in the Divinity of our Lord does not rest merely upon authority, — whether the authority of councils or of the original apostles. Under the illumination of the Holy Spirit, and as the result of the experience of the Christian life, Christian men, in one generation after another, see for themselves the glory of God in Christ Jesus our Lord.

So again with the doctrine of the Holy Spirit. Dr. Dale said he knew he was interpreting the experience of Christian men accurately when saying that we are conscious that it is in the strength of a Divine Power that we trust in the infinite love of God in Christ for the remission of sins, submit to His authority, and rejoice in His grace. But where there is a Divine Power there must always be a Divine Person; this is not an inference from experience, but a part of experience.

Again also when he comes to the great doctrine of the Atonement, he comes to fact and experience. He points out that in spite of the corruptions which have enfeebled the faith and dishonored the morals of the Church, this great truth, though often obscured, has never been dislodged from its place and authority in Christian thought. Theologians have given varying and conflicting explanations of it, but its power over the hearts of the faithful has remained unbroken. That the Death of Christ was a sacrifice for the sins of the world, and that through the blood of Christ we have the forgiveness of sins has been verified in the actual experience of the Christian Church. Nothing is more real than the sense of guilt, and when men have found no relief in tears and sorrow, or from attempts to amend their lives, they have seen that Christ had died for their sins, and then the shadow broke and passed away; the light of God shone upon them; they knew that they were forgiven. It is a wonderful experience, an experience that seems impossible until it is actually known; and then the reality of it is one of the great certainties of life. The blessedness of the remission of sin has been verified in the experience of Christian men through sixty generations.

In this living way Dr. Dale set forth Christian doctrine to the living men and women who gathered round his pulpit from week to week. "I find," he says, "'the pillar and ground of the truth' in the actual life of those who have received the Christian salvation. The biography of saints is a higher authority than the decrees of councils. . . . For me the doctrinal authority of the Church lies in the experience of the Church. Its experience constitutes its authority — the experience of the commonalty of those who have received the Christian redemption. . . . The actual experience of penitents and saints is sacred to me; when we are in immediate contact with the divine life of man, we are in contact with the presence and power of the Spirit of God. The 'Confessions' of Augustine are of more authority than his theological treatises; Bunyan's 'Grace Abounding' than Calvin's 'Institutes.' I believe in the inspiration of the Church, and I find that inspiration in its life."

And now let us pass from *substance* to *form* and *style*. Dr. Fairbairn has said that Dr. Dale's spoken discourse recalled the heroic age of the English sermon. This spoken discourse, so far as style is concerned, was largely influenced by that of Edmund Burke. From Dale's biography we learn that his admiration for Burke, which began at college, lasted on till his latest years. When sleepless nights were upon him, he had always a pile of books by his bedside, and invariably a volume or two of Burke might be found among them. Other books came and went, but Burke remained a faithful friend not to be dispossessed. In view of this fact, it is curious to notice how many points of similarity there were between the two men. Many of the things said by Hazlitt and John Morley about Burke might be said with almost equal truth about Dr. Dale. Hazlitt, comparing Burke with his great contemporary the Earl of Chatham, says that while Chatham's wisdom was altogether plain and practical, Burke's was profound and contemplative; while Chatham led men to *act*, Burke made them *think*; that while Chatham's eloquence roused the multitude and enabled him to wield their physical energy as he pleased, Burke's carried conviction into the mind of the retired and lonely student; and that while Chatham supplied his hearers with *motives* to immediate action, Burke furnished them with *reasons* for action, which might have little effect upon them at the time, but for which they would be wiser and better all their lives after. In short, if Burke did not produce the same effects on ordinary minds as some others have done, it was not from want of power, but because his subjects, his ideas, and his arguments were less common. John Morley, too, in his "Life of Burke," says that he combined his thoughts and knowledge in propositions of wisdom so weighty and strong that the minds of ordinary hearers were not on the instant prepared for them. Elsewhere also he says that in the coolest and dryest of Burke's writings there is the mark of greatness, of grasp, of comprehension; that he had the style of his subjects, the amplitude, the weightiness, the grandeur proper to a man dealing with imperial themes, — the freedom of nations, the justice of rulers, the fortunes of great societies, the sacredness of law.

If we pass over from the domain of political philosophy to that of theology, the substance of what is here said about Burke might be applied without reserve to Dr. Dale. Upon all *his* best work, too, there is the mark of greatness, of grasp and comprehension; and no one can read the books he has left us without feeling that he had the style of his subjects, — the amplitude, the weightiness, the grandeur proper to a man dealing with great and sacred themes. It is because he is such an admirable example of literary style, because his sermons were literature rather than sermons, that I wish to make use of him to raise a very practical and important question of interest to all preachers. The question is this: Even if a man can attain to a very high degree of excellence in a purely literary style, is it the most effective form of pulpit address? May it not be that the very qualities which are excellencies in literature may prove drawbacks to spoken discourse? Almost the same things have been said of both these men. Hazlitt was of opinion that Burke's writings are better than his speeches, and that indeed his speeches are writings. Similarly Dr. Fairbairn says that Dr. Dale's words, "though written to be spoken, are even more fitted to be read than to be heard; for his books are as firm in texture, as weighty in matter, as vigorous in expression as the concentrated thought of a strong man could make them." So far as public speech is concerned, how far may this compact literary style be said to be a success? Let us take first the one man and then the other for the purpose of this inquiry.

John Morley, as his latest biographer, is of opinion that though as an orator Burke was transcendent, yet in that immediate influence upon his hearers which is commonly supposed to be the mark of oratorical success, all the evidence is that he generally failed. Perhaps the greatest speech he ever made was that on conciliation with America: the wisest in its temper, the most closely logical in its reasoning, the amplest in its appropriate topics, the most generous and conciliating in the substance of its appeals. Yet, as a matter of fact, Erskine, who was in the House when it was delivered, said that it drove everybody away, including people who, when they came to read it, read it over and over again, and could hardly think of anything else. Burke is held forth as a memorable instance of more than adequate means of commanding success resulting in a very inadequate share of it. The greatest political philosopher of his day, he yet commanded no adherents; the greatest orator, he yet commanded no converts, and could scarce command an audience. He was the best-informed man in Parliament, the most exact and ready in his information. In addition, he had the means of pleasing as well as convincing; for his language was choice and classical and copiously various, while imagery the most bountiful and most beautiful set off his homeliest wares. Yet we are told that he was tiresome, that his name passed into a parliamentary proverb, and that the signal for his rising to speak was the signal for his audience to quit their benches. It is clear from this conspicuous instance that literature and spoken discourse are not quite the same thing. The spoken discourse meant to be heard and the written composition intended to be read, should be prepared on widely different lines. Otherwise such qualities as profundity of thought, closeness and consecutiveness of reasoning, elaborated with refinement and beauty of style, may seriously mar the effectiveness of what is addressed to the ear. For if a man who is reading a book cannot quite follow the writer's argument, he can turn back and go over the paragraph again. But the man who is hearing a speech or a sermon must understand it at the first hearing or not at all. It has been well said that an average audience cannot be fed with intellectual pemmican. It is a form of food too concentrated for general use. Therefore what is tiresome in a book may be desirable in a sermon. Without ceasing to be vivacious and interesting, the argument may proceed at somewhat slower pace; the same thought may be presented in varied language and diversified aspects; and there is larger room for the use of pictorial forms and familiar illustrations. The speaker should make sure as he goes along not only that the ideas are there, but that they are presented in the way best calculated to strike and tell.

In the case of Dr. Dale, the admirable biography given us by his son deals with this question of his style quite frankly, and, so far as preachers are concerned, seems to me one of the most interesting and instructive parts of the book. In a footnote to one of the pages a portion of a letter is quoted from one of Dr. Dale's most intelligent hearers, in which the writer says: "In my own estimation he always ranked higher as a teacher than a preacher of the truth. If I read a sermon which I had previously heard him preach, it always proved superior to what was expected. The delivery had too little variety of tone, and was too impassioned, as a rule, and until his later years was destitute of pathos." The defects in delivery, this gentleman points out, may be traced, I think, to Dr. Dale's style of composition. A close, compact, and weighty style of writing leads almost necessarily to monotony of delivery and lack of pathos. It leaves too little room for play of tone and feeling.

It must not, however, be inferred from what has been said that Dr. Dale did not often produce almost sublime effects even with this condensed literary style of his. It is now thirty years ago, but I vividly remember the profound impression created by his address on "Christ and the Controversies of Christendom," delivered from the Chair of the Congregational Union. A friend of mine also who heard him preach his great sermon on "The Theology of John Wesley," in connection with the celebration of the centenary of John Wesley's death, told me that the effect of the sermon upon that great audience was, at certain points, simply overwhelming. It seemed as if the people would rise to their feet and give vent to their feelings in excited acclaim. Of course the occasion was special, and so was the audience. Then, too, the more abstract parts of the sermon were broken up by passages of historical narrative, in addition to which there was much that was concrete in the setting forth of the religious experience of the Founder of Methodism. It will be seen at once that the ordinary conditions of a Sunday after Sunday ministry are necessarily different from those of a special service such as I have referred to. And while no one can doubt for a moment that Dr. Dale's regular ministrations among his own people were effective and instructive in a high degree to many of his hearers, he himself seems to have felt that the elaborate literary style he had acquired, and which had become part of himself, and which has made his books so valued a possession to the Church of God, was, to some extent, a drawback to his usefulness as a preacher. His self-revelations on this point, as given in his biography, seem to me very instructive.

In a letter to his colleague and senior, the Rev. John Angell James, written some three years after his settlement in Birmingham, he says: "'The present church and congregation are on the whole, I believe, more than satisfied with my ministry. Many are personally attached to me and believe that they derive strength and instruction from my ministry. . . . On the other hand: but twelve or fifteen months ago there was very considerable dissatisfaction on the part of the wisest, strongest, and best people in the Church, occasioned by my preaching doctrines which I still hold, and by the influence on my ministry of mental and moral habits too deeply rooted ever to be wholly destroyed."

Farther on in the same letter he confides to Mr. James that his most cherished ambition had been to gather a congregation of his own from the artisan class, and he says: "Sadly but slowly, I have come to the conviction that I cannot do it. My preaching must always be to a large extent speculative and doctrinal. To reconstruct one's mind and completely transform one's habits is hard, almost an impossible task. Such men as Mr. Beaumont — whose head appears to me to be one of the finest I ever met with — complained that it was hard work to follow my sermons on 'Romans.' Wherever I go, I must strive against the excessive tendency to abstractions by which my preaching must have been characterized for such a man to speak so of it."

Thirty years later circumstances led to his returning to the subject again. The occasion was this: there had been a Church Fellowship Conference in his congregation, at which one of the members read a paper offering suggestions as to what could be done to contribute to the strength and efficiency of their Church life. He began with the pulpit, and the conversation at which Dr. Dale was present was very much arrested at this first part of the paper. Kindness was the dominant element of the criticism offered, and it was cheerfully granted that their minister's sermons had intellectual, literary, and spiritual qualities which commanded the sympathy and gratitude of the best and most cultivated of his hearers. At the same time it was urged by several that Dr. Dale's preaching moved at a height — intellectual and spiritual — far above that of the congregation generally.

This conference took place a short time before he left home for quiet sojourn at his country house by the sea. He now for the first time began to keep a diary in which to write his thoughts about himself and his work, and this is what he says as to the course of the conversation at the Church Conference in question: "I have been thinking much, and with much concern about my preaching. It has a fatal defect. It is wanting in an element which is indispensable to real success. I do not think that I should state the exact truth if I said that I was not anxious for the conversion and perfection of individual men, and cared only for setting forth the truth. But I fear that the truth occupies too large a place in my thought, and that I have been too much occupied with the instrument — the divine instrument — for effecting the ends of the ministry."

On this important point of effectively getting hold of the people he says further: "I felt rather strongly towards the close of last year that in one respect among others my ministry — especially of late years — had been gravely defective. I have striven to press home upon men and to illustrate the very central contents of Christ's Gospel; but I have not recognized practically the obligation to use in preaching all those secondary powers which contribute to create and sustain intellectual and emotional interest in preaching. The more strenuous intellectual effort in order to make truth clear, and put it strongly, has not been neglected; but there has not been the legitimate use, either in the choice of subjects or their treatment, of those elements which are of a rhetorical character, and which raise the audience into a condition which is perhaps friendly to the reception of Christian truth. I have a dread of aiming at the 'popular' method of treatment, arising from a dread of aiming at 'popularity,' but the two aims are wholly distinct, and it has been a fault not to aim at the first."

Yet again he has a significant sentence or two in reference to his style. He says: "The word which has been often used to denote what critics regarded as the excellence of my preaching and speaking really suggested the qualities in which both had been defective, and the preaching more than the speaking — '*stateliness*.' That is not the characteristic of effective preaching; and it suggests a whole set of intellectual, ethical, and spiritual elements which account for failure."

So we come to this: the lesson other preachers may learn from Dr. Dale's self-revelations is that *stateliness* of style, elaborate literary finish, even in the hands of a master, is *not* the most effective style for the pulpit. That which may make a man's work good as literature may mar it for spoken discourse. At the same time it does not follow, on the other hand, because a public speaker had better not put on the stiff brocade of stateliness, that he must needs fall into a style loose and slipshod. Some of the greatest masters of speech sufficiently prove the contrary. John Bright's speeches, for instance, have, by some of the ablest judges, been admitted to be among the noblest examples of oratory in our time; yet though often characterized by eloquence and even grandeur, no one would say they had the defect and drawback of stateliness; and certainly they were never loose or slipshod. They were never below the dignity or the importance of the subject on the one hand; and they never overstrained the minds of the audience on the other. There were familiar passages which gave a sense of rest to the hearer, and also passages which at times bore him along on the current of strong emotion. Variety, unexpectedness, interest, instruction were so blended with convincing argument, touching pathos, and stirring appeal, that the audience were only sorry at the end that all was over. This leads me to say, in conclusion, that for preachers such speeches are better models of style than the most stately sermons, or the most elaborate compositions of the great masters in literature.

IX

REPRESENTATIVE PREACHERS OF MODERN PURITANISM

III. DR. ALEXANDER MACLAREN

LECTURE IX

REPRESENTATIVE PREACHERS OF MODERN PURITANISM

III. DR. ALEXANDER MACLAREN

THE three preachers I have already brought to your notice, as typical representatives of Modern Puritanism in our own century, have all passed from the ranks of the living to the higher service. In this concluding lecture I should like to set before you one man in the English pulpit of to-day, still spared to us, — long may he be spared, — whose career as a minister and whose methods as a preacher seem to me more than usually suggestive to younger men. I refer to Dr. Alexander Maclaren of Manchester, whose sermons are, I believe, almost as well known in America as they are in England. It so happens that before going to my present pastorate in Bedford I was, for six years of his Manchester life, minister of another church in the same city, and am therefore able, from personal knowledge to some extent, to speak of the beginnings of his work in the sphere he has served and adorned so long. From 1858 to the present time, a period of more than forty years, his intellectual and spiritual influence as a preacher, in one of the foremost of English cities, has never wavered or waned.

I hesitate to apply the word "popularity" in his case simply because it is an equivocal word and has come to be applied to men of whose methods one cannot always think with pleasure. We may, however, use it in Dr. Maclaren's case in the noblest sense, for his popularity is based upon solid and lasting foundations, has been won by legitimate means, and is such as all good men can unfeignedly rejoice over. He instinctively shrinks from everything that may be called playing to the gallery, and declines to lower his own ideal for the sake of securing the favor of his audience. His unbroken career as a minister for more than half a century, his marvellous instructive and incisive power as a preacher, make him and his method of more than ordinary interest to those whose vocation is to be that of the preacher. Let me try to show what we may learn from him.

In 1846, at the early age of twenty, Alexander Maclaren went from college to be minister of a comparatively small congregation on a very modest stipend in the town of Southampton. There is this to be noted, that though the congregation was small at starting, he felt it to be worthy of the best he could give to it. He held faithfully and tenaciously to his work, and there is no better way of turning a small place into a large one than that of making the most of it and doing your best to it while you are in it. He occasionally took up work aside from his main line of service. During that first pastorate he found time to lecture to the general public of the town on such subjects as "John Milton's Prose Writings," "Martin Luther," "John Knox," "The Covenanters of Scotland," "Realized Utopias," and "The Wisdom of Boldness." But he never neglected the pulpit for the lecture hall or the platform. First of all, and above all things else, he was a preacher of the Eternal Word. The survivors of his Southampton congregation, while willing to admit that he is more forceful and more cultured in the 'nineties than he was in the 'fifties, still contend that he has never reached higher levels than he frequently did in the days when he was their minister. The result of honest, steadfast, painstaking work in that early pastorate was such that at the end of twelve years he left at Southampton a congregation which filled the church building; and he took with him to Manchester an established reputation as one of the ablest, most interesting, and most instructive of Nonconformist preachers.

This preliminary word about Dr. Maclaren will probably make you willing to know more about his style of preaching and his methods of work. Let us begin with his method of preparation first, and, of course, on this he himself can give us the most reliable information. He says: "I began my ministry with the resolution that I would not write sermons, but would think and feel them, and I have stuck to it ever since. It costs quite as much time in preparation as writing, and a far greater expenditure of nervous energy in delivery; but I am sure that it is best for me, and equally sure that everybody has to find out his own way." Going more into detail he says: "I write my sermons in part. The amount of written matter varies. When I can, I like to write a couple of sentences or so of introduction, in order to get a fair start, and for the rest I content myself with jottings, fragmentary hints of a word or two each, interspersed here and there with a fully written sentence. Illustrations and metaphors I never write. A word suffices for them. If I have 'heads' I word these carefully, and I like to write the closing sentences. That is my ideal, a sufficiently scrappy one you will think, but I seldom attain to it, and am most frequently obliged to preach with much less preparation. The amount written varies from about six or seven pages of ordinary note paper — widely written into short lines, each line only holding a word or two — to the barest skeleton, that would go in half a page. I do not adhere to what is written, as there is very little of it sufficiently consecutive. I make no attempt to reproduce more than the general course of thought, and constantly find that the best bits of my sermon make themselves in preaching. I do adhere to my introductory sentences, which serve to shove me off into deep water; but beyond that, I let the moment shape the thing. Expressions I do not prepare. If I can get the fire alight, that is what I care for most."

Such is Dr. Maclaren's own account of himself. Probably young beginners would be afraid to trust themselves to such daring methods as these at first, just as young swimmers would be afraid to trust themselves in deep waters at the start. Even in the case of Dr. Maclaren himself, one who has long known him, tells us that in his earlier time his fastidiousness in the choice of words led often to long pauses, which lasted till he found fitting expression for his thought and that the refusal to accept any but the best language in which to clothe his ideas goes far to explain his skill in the use of the choicest English. Further, that his mode of preparation had this effect sometimes, that his material did not always last as long as he expected. In such cases, when his wool was done, he had the courage to leave off spinning. He would never condescend to empty talk merely for the sake of filling up what has come to be regarded as the canonical time. He has been known to sit down at the end of twelve minutes, simply remarking that he had no more to say. And I do not know why a minister should go on talking when he has no more to say, though there are some ministers who do.

And now let us look still more closely into Dr. Maclaren's methods, and ascertain if we can the secret of his substantial and long-continued success. We shall have to assume, as taken for granted, very much of personal sort, — his natural endowment, his keen intellect, and that intense nervous force which quickens and intensifies all his thinking and speaking. These are the gifts from Heaven, the sovereign bestowal with which he started life. Every man hath his own proper gift, of which we say he hath nothing which he hath not received, and of which it is true that "a man's gift maketh room for him." All this, I say, we take for granted, and we are now concerned rather with the use the man has made of the gifts with which he set out in life.

In the forefront of the causes of Dr. Maclaren's success as a preacher, I should be disposed to place the fact that his teaching is firmly based upon and is a careful exposition of the revelation God has given to us in the Scriptures. Beyond most men, he seems to have resolved that his one mission shall be to make clear to men's understandings, and to bring home to men's hearts, the mind of the Spirit of God as given to us in the Word of God. All through his public life he has continued to be a careful student of the original languages of Scripture, and his popular teaching is based upon an accurate examination of the grammatical structure of every text he takes. The text is never used as a mere motto for the sermon, but the sermon is an exact exposition of the text. The context is taken into careful account; each word has its due place in arriving at the meaning of the whole; and the niceties of distinction between the different tenses of the verb are duly recognized. Yet all this takes place in no mere pedantic fashion. The preacher is no slave to grammar and lexicon; but when he has laid his foundation in absolute verity, the superstructure raised thereupon is instinct with life and soul. Every man who listens to him may feel quite sure that the meaning he gives is, so far as he can find it, honestly brought out of Scripture and not unlawfully thrust into it. If he ever takes a text simply by way of accommodation, which he very rarely does, he frankly tells his audience that he is doing so, and at the same time he seems half-disposed to apologize for the fact. On one occasion, for example, he took for the subject of his sermon the chambers of imagery spoken of by the prophet Ezekiel, and started by saying: "Now I take this text in a meaning which the prophet had no intention to put on it. I do not often do that with my texts, and when I do I like to confess frankly that I am doing it. And so I take the words as a kind of symbol which may help to put into, perhaps, a picturesque and more striking form some very familiar and homely truths." After thus frankly putting himself right with his audience, he then proceeded to use Ezekiel's vision as symbolizing the dark painted chamber in men's hearts, the idolatries that go on there, and the way that Heaven's light is sometimes flashed into the midst of these idolatries. He seems to hold Scripture as much too sacred a thing to be used merely for popular effect, or the display of oratory. I cannot conceive of him making use of it for purposes of personal vanity by showing how cleverly he can bring out a meaning from an obscure text which no one ever suspected to be in it, and which was probably not in it. The mere suggestion of such a thing would, I think, give him pain. If ever a prophet of God stood in the midst of our modern nineteenth century life with the burden of God upon his heart, and a "Thus saith the Lord" upon his lips, this preacher of whom I am speaking is that prophet.

His intelligent reverence for Scripture is accompanied with, or rather grows out of, his firm belief in the historical facts related in Scripture. Human speculations which change with the changing years are with him as the small dust of the balance when placed by the side of that Word of the Living God which abideth forever. Take, for example, that central fact of Scripture, the resurrection of our Lord from the dead. This to Dr. Maclaren is as certain as any of the facts of ancient or modern history. For his part he is sure that if that resurrection had not taken place we should have heard no more of Jesus and his religion than we do of John the Baptist, after his disciples took him up and buried him. He is confident that if there had been no resurrection of Christ, there would have been no Church of Christ. So sure is he of the fact in question, that even if he consented to yield up everything that the most craving and unreasonable modern scepticism can demand concerning the date and authority of the books of the New Testament, he would be content to rest the matter on the evidence contained in the four Epistles of Paul, the genuineness of which no one has ever questioned. In his view, next to proclaiming the

Gospel, the main work of the Apostles was not to pass on spiritual power and authority in one unbroken chain of Apostolical Succession, but to be personal witnesses of the resurrection of Christ. That one fact with its consequences formed the substance of the first sermon recorded in the Acts of the Apostles so far as the Twelve are concerned; and Paul in his turn delivered unto his hearers, first of all, that which he also received, that Christ died for our sins, was buried, and had been raised again on the third day. In this preacher's belief, as in Paul's, there is nothing but that message between us and the darkness of despair.

Further, he is equally sure that the death which preceded that resurrection was in a real, profound, and far-reaching sense an Atonement for the sin of the world, a means of Reconciliation between God and man. All the agony of Gethsemane, and all the striking peculiarities of the death on the Cross are to him inexplicable except on this understanding. For him the Cross of Christ reveals to the world for all time, and for eternity too, a love which shrinks from no sacrifices; a love which is capable of the most entire abandonment; a love which is diffused over the whole surface of humanity, and through all ages; a love which comes laden with the richest and highest gifts, even the turning of selfish and sinful hearts into its own pure and perfect likeness. It is all this because in that death something is done which was not completed by the life, however fair, by the words, however wise and tender, by the works of power, however restorative and healing. Here is something more than these present. What more? This more, that His Cross is the propitiation for the sins of the whole world. Take up Dr. Maclaren's sermons when and where you will, in his earliest as in his latest ministry, — there is no hesitation, no wavering, even for a moment, on this central and most vital matter. In his inmost soul so sure is he that the death on the Cross effected something real and permanent for the salvation of the world, that he declares, again and again, that if any preacher leaves this out of his message his ministry will be futile and fruitless. To use his own expression, a Christianity without a dying Christ is a dying Christianity.

To pass on another step: What has impressed me very powerfully about Dr. Maclaren's preaching is its intensely *practical* character, and that, too, in a special and somewhat unusual sense of the word. Let me explain what I mean, for I lay much stress upon his preaching as a model for all preachers in this one respect.

When we speak of *practical preaching*, we usually associate with the words the idea of ethical instruction in the duties of daily life, or an attempt to deal with the social problems of our time. But this is not the precise idea which is in my mind just now. Here and there in the sermons I am reviewing you will find incisive and instructive utterances on these subjects. But I have an impression that so far as social problems are concerned this preacher is of opinion that if you could get men made right within — spiritually right — it would not be long before social problems would right themselves. When therefore I describe Dr. Maclaren's sermons as practical preaching, I attach a much profounder meaning to the words than that of mere guidance in the matter of ethical duty. I mean thereby clear and definite instruction as to the rationale of the divine life in the souls of men, — its nature, its beginnings, its after-developments, and the spiritual forces by which it is begun and carried on. I quite recognize the fact that other preachers deal with such questions as these, — many of them ably and to the advantage of their people. But I am not able to recall any other preacher, either of Puritan or modern times, so clearly constructive in his teachings on the New Life Christ came to give us. There is surely what may be called a science of the spiritual life, dealing with the facts and forces of the inner world as revealed from God, and verified and confirmed by the experience of man. What is this life? How do we get it? In what way is it related to the already existing life? Along what lines is it developed, and by what supernatural forces? Heaven-illumined and carefully thought-out instruction on matters so vital and practical is always needed, and will always be welcomed by the most earnest-minded of our people. Some kind of teaching is called for which shall be equally removed from the shallow, easy-going platitudes of the mere revivalist on the one hand, and the too vague, commonplace utterances of many ordinary preachers on the other. And it is here, as it seems to me, that Dr. Maclaren's distinctive excellence as a preacher shows itself. Through a long public life he has been a continuous, profound, accurate, and prayerful student of God's revelation, and at the same time a close observer of the actual facts of religious experience as found in the living men and women who make up the Church of God to-day. In this way, so far as the nature of the subject permits, he has attained to something like a clear and coherent science of that spiritual life which is derived from Christ and maintained in the soul by the Spirit of God; and, as we might expect, this science underlies all his teachings. Let me try to show this in briefest manner and in merest outline.

Dr. Maclaren finds both in Scripture teaching and in the facts of actual life a real and unmistakable contrast between what we may call the natural man and the spiritual; or, to use another Pauline expression, between the old man which waxeth corrupt after the lusts that deceive, and the new man which, after God, has been created in righteousness and holiness of truth. Under all superficial differences a Christless life is neither more nor less than a life shaped according to and under the influence of those passionate desires in our nature which were meant to be the driving power, but not the guiding power. Given the immense variety of tastes, likings, and desires which men have, the point and characteristic feature of every godless life is that, be these what they may, they become the dominant power in that life. There may, of course, be every now and then remonstrances of conscience, considerations of prudence, occasional dim desires after something better; but apart from Christ it is not conscience that rules the life; it is not the sense of duty that is strongest, — the real directing impulse to which the inward proclivities, if not the outward activities yield in the man, is, — the things that we like, the passionate desires of nature, the sensuous and godless heart. Yet the fact remains, as I have already intimated, that these likes and dislikes, these passionate desires of nature were never meant to be men's guides. They were meant to be impulses having motive power; but the destruction of all true manhood comes of their being made the directing power. Things must be kept in their right places, and the divine order stands thus: lowest down are the strong impulses of our nature; above them, the enlightened understanding; above that, the conscience; and above that again, God Himself, irradiating and hallowing all. In the case of the unspiritual man, this order is reversed. The depravity of his nature does not mean that there is no good in him, that in every form of evil he has gone the greatest lengths he could, — but that the bent of his nature is wrong — he is ruled by his natural desires. And the thing to be noted is that these desires deceive the man, never yielding the satisfaction they promise; and they corrupt as well as deceive. The spiritual nature is gradually destroyed by the eating leprosy of sin.

The facts being thus, the practical question arises, How is all this to be changed? How shall the old nature, corrupt according to the desires that deceive, become the new nature which, after God, is created in righteousness and holiness of truth? The new man is not our work, it is God's creation. But how is it brought about? The answer is — by the reception of a new life from above, a life from Christ imparted to the soul through the avenue of a trusting faith, and by the mysterious action of the Spirit of God. The past is blotted out by forgiveness, and a new force is started to be the force of the future. The law of the Spirit of life in Christ Jesus sets the man free from the law of sin and of death.

But now as to the part which the man himself has to take in the matter, how does he get this life? The answer given is that which comes from Christ Himself — "by Faith that is in *Me.*" Thus the starting-point is reached, which is faith, — personal trust in a personal Saviour. When it is said that faith saves a man, this is true and yet not true. It is not faith which saves, but that to which faith clings. It is Christ that saves. Faith is simply the hand that takes the gift, the channel along which the water of life flows into the soul. If it were not for the gift, the hand would be nothing; if it were not for the water, the channel would be useless. Faith saves by getting a living hold of the Christ who saves. The object of faith is not a creed, but a Person, whom it is the work of the creeds to make known to us, since we cannot trust without knowing something about Him whom we trust. And the Person thus made known is not merely one who is set forth as our example or teacher. The Christ, trusting in whom is salvation, is the Christ whose blood cleanses from all sin, whose righteousness makes us righteous — Christ Himself in the sweetness and graciousness of His character, but also in the sacrifice of His death and in the glory of His risen life. This is the Christ, trusting in whom we live.

The value of faith then consists in the grandeur and fulness of the object to which faith is directed. And as for faith itself, it is not something occult and mysterious which belongs to the sphere of religion and is found nowhere else. It is strictly parallel with the trust which we have in one another in daily life. The feeling which knits us to Christ, and to God in Christ, is the same as that which knits us to one another, and which makes it possible that the world should go on at all. The same confidence which men have with one another in business, the same confidence with which we, in our families, safely trust in the love and truth of wife or husband, friend or child, when directed to Jesus Christ, becomes the spring and heart of all religion.

The union thus brought about by this trust between Christ and the soul carries with it two results, — one dealing with the past, the other with the future. It brings with it the forgiveness of sin and the transformation of the one life into the likeness of the other. The forgiveness of sin is a real thing to the man, a veritable blotting out of transgression.

This is something more than the remission of penalty, the deliverance from condemnation; though all this is most surely in it. It extends to the removal of all hindrances to the outflow of our heavenly Father's love, and to the actual communication of that love as being the very heart of His forgiveness to us. Notwithstanding the black barrier which we have flung across the stream by our sin, the pure and deep flood of the love of God rises and surges over the impediment and fills our souls. This forgiveness does away with the penalty of sin. What is that penalty? The wages of sin is death, — the wrenching away of a dependent soul from God, — your sins have *separated* between you and God. How is that penalty ended? By the union of the soul with God in a threefold bond of trust, love, and obedience. The real penalty, which is separation from God, passes away when the love is welcomed and received. The outward consequences of sin in the life may still remain to humble the man and make him watchful. A man who has been immoral in the past may have to carry the consequences of his sin with him in his body to the grave, and yet be a forgiven man. For our worst sins, there is plenteous redemption, and yet our least sins may, in our lives, our characters, our memories, our consciences, our worldly position, reputation, and health, leave their traces and consequences.

Such, so far as the past is concerned, is the result of faith in Christ to the soul that trusts. There is also further result. Christ comes and lives in that man. There is a divine indwelling of Christ in the man by His Spirit. Just as light and beauty travel into the soul through the eye, and the harmonies of music through the ear, so through the avenues of trust and love comes Christ by His Spirit into the innermost depths of the life. And this is an indwelling which fits for further indwelling. Christ in the heart makes the heart more fit for Christ. If we let Him in, He makes us temples meet for Himself. The indwelling issues in transformation. As iron near a magnet becomes magnetic, so souls in which Christ dwells become Christlike. The likeness extends, becomes deeper, truer, every way more perfect; comprehends more and more of the faculties of the man; enters into him until he is saturated with the glory; and in all the extent of his being, and in all the depth possible to each part of that whole extent, is like his Lord. That is the hope for heaven, towards which we may indefinitely approximate here, and at which we shall absolutely arrive there.

Such, in brief and as gathered from various discourses, is Dr. Maclaren's putting of the facts of the spiritual life in man, — what that life is, how it comes, how it is developed, and to what issues it tends. No doubt much of what I have stated sounds familiar enough, yet few indeed are the preachers who have made the laws of that life so clear to our apprehension, so living, so real, who have studied them with such keen insight of human intelligence joined to such depth of divine illumination.

Then, too, not only so far as the substance of his teaching is concerned, does this great preacher of our own time serve as a model to us, but also in the crystal clearness of his way of putting the truth before the minds of his audience. His first aim seems to be to see straight into the very heart of the subject before him. He makes what is most vital and central stand out with most distinctness. He does not burden the mind or distract the attention by too many details, and he so arranges his thoughts that, in the most natural manner, one part of the subject prepares the way for that which is to follow. So that it must be a dull mind indeed which cannot follow him along the path he travels. He never descends to little tricks or devices in stating the divisions of his sermon. His sole aim, evidently, is to present the truth in its very simplest form. These divisions are serious and seriously meant, and they are arranged in such manner as to show that one of the clearest and most far-seeing intellects has been keenly at work. By way of illustration, take his sermon on the text (Rom. viii. 17): "If children then heirs, heirs of God and joint-heirs with Christ." Premising first that God Himself is His own greatest gift, and that the richest blessing we can receive is to be made heirs of God, possessors of God in the only way one person can possess another, by love and living intercourse, he proceeds to point out the conditions upon which the possession of this great inheritance depends. He shows that in the condensed utterance of the text we have the following series of truths: There is no inheritance without sonship; there is no sonship without a spiritual birth; there is no spiritual birth without Christ; there is no Christ for us without faith. Such is his lucid way of putting things. It is the great merit of Dr. Maclaren's preaching that the most ordinary minds can follow him with interest from first to last, and at the same time the most intellectual feel, on after-reflection, that there was more in what they heard than they saw at the time. Speaking generally, there are in his sermons no ragged edges, no confusions of thought, no signs of struggle as of a man making his way through mental fog. You feel as you listen that this preacher has mastered his subject, has clearly seen his way right through before he stood up there face to face with the people. Addressing himself to preachers, he once said: "Don't try to be eloquent or mind very much about words." But he himself is eloquent without trying to be, — eloquent with the eloquence of strong conviction and clearly ascertained truth.

And I must not fail to notice that the great literary and intellectual qualities of this man are suffused with intense spiritual earnestness, — earnestness which is not merely assumed for the hour he stands up there, but which is of a piece with his whole life. During the few times I have had the opportunity of hearing him in his own church, I have come away from the midst of the crowd pouring through the doorways, feeling that it must be a solemn responsibility for any congregation to listen constantly to such preaching as that. Either it must lead to great enlightenment and elevation of character, or to great callousness of soul, according as it is received or rejected. The explanation of this man's power is that he dwells in the secret place of the Most High and abides under the shadow of the Almighty. In the most unaffected way, he tells us: "I have always found that my own comfort and efficiency in preaching have been in direct proportion to the frequency and depth of daily communion with God. I know no way in which we can do our work but in quiet fellowship with Him; in resolutely keeping up the habits of the student's life, which needs some power of saying, *No;* and by conscientious pulpit preparation. The secret of success in everything is trust in God and hard work."

In these direct and manly words you have the spirit of this man's life and the secret of his success. How much of spiritual good has been accomplished under God by this honored and faithful ministry of now more than fifty years, no man knows. You can no more tabulate spiritual results than you can weigh the fragrance of flowers in scales, or the beauty of the landscape in a balance. But the day shall declare it. And in that day "they that be wise shall shine as the brightness of the firmament; and they that turn many to righteousness as the stars for ever and ever."

To-day I bring my task to a close and take my leave of you. It would gladden me much to think that I had been in any degree honored of God to exalt your ideal of the ministry, and strengthen a worthy ambition to be found faithful therein. I congratulate you on the career which may open up before you as ministers of Christ when your studies in this place have reached their end. If I may allow myself a personal reference, I would say, after nearly five and forty years spent in the Congregational ministry, were life to begin again I could wish it to be spent along the same pleasant path of honorable service, with this difference, that it might be more faithfully spent. The work never seemed so great as it does now, — now as the shadow lengthens on the plain, and the day wears on to evensong.

As one by one you leave the college gates

at the end of your college course, to think of something like forty or fifty years' service ahead may seem like looking along an inexhaustible vista of time. You will be surprised hereafter, if spared, to find how quickly all these years are gone. With all your heart throw yourselves into your work from the first. You will find it deepen in interest. Apart from your public service, or rather growing out of it, your lives will become intertwined with other lives in the most sacred relationships. You will be with your people, not only in sanctuary worship, but also in all the varied scenes of personal and family life. You will be with them, not only along the quiet levels of routine, but also in times when God is dealing closest with them, in hours of great sorrows and deep heart experiences, when it seems as if all God's waves and billows were going over them. It is at such times that the most sacred ties are formed. As you enter with brotherly sympathy into the various joys and sorrows of their life, your people will grow to be much to you, — how much you will never know till you are called to leave them, or they to leave you. An apostle of Christ who was a true shepherd of souls in the olden time, spoke of the people to whom he had ministered in the Gospel as "my brethren beloved and longed-for, my joy and crown." "For what is our hope, or joy or crown of glorying? Are not even ye, before our Lord Jesus at His coming? For ye are our glory and joy."

In saying farewell to you, let me leave this good wish for you, that you may have many years of happy service among a people knit to your hearts by ties as sacred as these thus exultingly set forth; and at the end may both they and you be numbered with God's saints in glory everlasting!